Illinois

Mapping the Prairie State through History

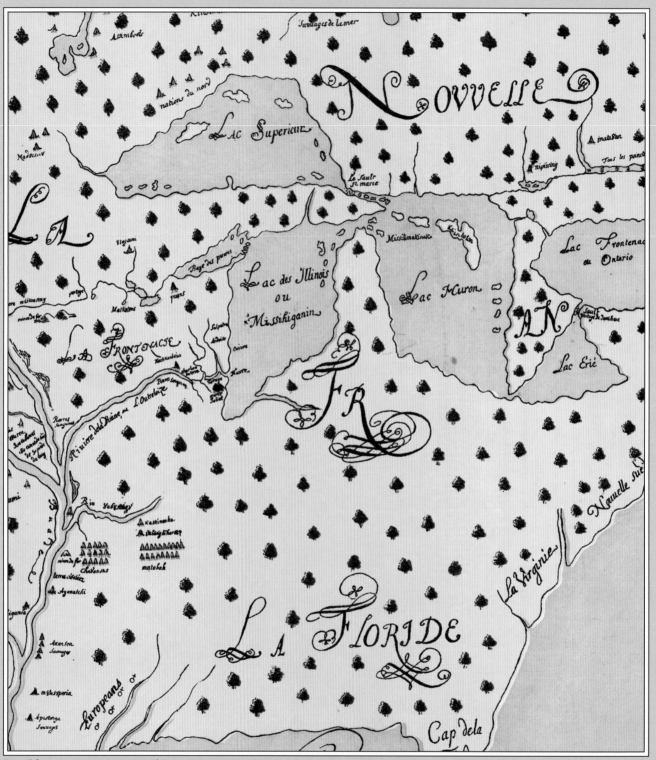

Detail from map on pages 4 and 5

Illinois

MAPPING THE PRAIRIE STATE THROUGH HISTORY

Rare and Unusual Maps from the Library of Congress

Vincent Virga

and Scotti Cohn

Guilford, Connecticut

Text design: Sheryl P. Kober
Project editor: Julie Marsh
Layout and Photoshop artist: Casey Shain

Library of Congress Cataloging-in-Publication Data

Virga, Vincent.
  Illinois, mapping the prairie state through history : rare and unusual maps from the Library of Congress / Vincent Virga and Scotti Cohn.
      p. cm.
  Includes bibliographical references.
  ISBN 978-0-7627-6011-4
  1. Illinois—Maps. 2. Historical geography—Illinois—Maps. 3. Atlases. I. Cohn, Scotti. II. Title.
  G1405.V6 2011
  911'.773—dc22

                                                        2010022991

Printed in China

10 9 8 7 6 5 4 3 2 1

Contents

Foreword

I KNEW ILLINOIS WAS A LONG STATE. HOWEVER, when Scotti Cohn informed me in her enlightening history that it extends farther north than Windsor, Ontario, and farther south than Richmond, Virginia, I went breathless! Who knew? Illinois is Lincoln, Obama, and Wyatt Earp; it's Al Capone and Hull House, Richard Wrights' Bigger Thomas, the "Chicago school" of architecture—the first to create what we call "skyscrapers"—and a sublime symphony orchestra. But I thought this cultural realm, our "Prairie State," was *flat*. Again, Scotti brought me back to Earth. Illinois has a huge variety of landscapes, a variety matched by our maps: "The maps in this book expand and enrich our understanding of when, how, and why Illinois became the remarkable place it is."

Living on planet Earth has always raised certain questions from those of us so inclined. Of course, the most obvious one is: Where am I? Well, as Virginia Woolf sagely noted in her diary, writing things down makes them more real; this may have been a motivating factor for the Old Stone Age artists who invented the language of signs on the walls of their caves in southern France and northern Spain between thirty-seven thousand and eleven thousand years ago. Picasso reportedly said, "They've invented everything," which includes the very concept of an image.

A map is an image. It makes the world more real for us and uses signs to create an essential sense of place in our imagination. (The petroglyphic maps that were inscribed in the late Iron Age on boulders high in the Valcamonica region of northern Italy are early examples of such signs.) Cartographic imaginings not only locate us on this Earth but also help us invent our personal and social identities, since maps embody our social order. Like the movies, maps helped create our national identity—though cinema had a vastly wider audience—and this encyclopedic series of books aims to make manifest the changing social order that invented the United States, which is why it embraces all fifty states.

Each is a precious link in the chain of events that is the history of our "great experiment," the first and enduring federal government ingeniously deriving its just powers—as John Adams proposed—from the consent of the governed. Each state has a physical presence that holds a unique 150place in any representation of our republic in maps. To see each one rise from the body of the continent conjures Tom Paine's excitement over the resourcefulness, the fecundity, the creative energy of our Enlightenment philosopher-founders: "We are brought at once to the point of seeing government begin, as if we had lived in the beginning of time." Just as the creators systemized not only laws but also rights in our constitution, so our maps show how their collective memory inspired the body politic to organize, codify, classify all of Nature to do their bidding with passionate preferences state by state. For they knew, as did Alexander Pope:

> All are but parts of one
>
> stupendous Whole
>
> Whose body Nature is,
>
> and God the soul.

And aided by the way maps under interrogation often evoke both time and space, we editors and historians have linked the reflective historical overviews of our nation's genesis to the seduction of place embedded in the art and science of cartography.

On October 9, 1492, after sailing westward for four weeks in an incomprehensibly vast and unknown sea, an anxious Christopher Columbus spotted an unidentified flock of migrating birds flying south and signifying land—"Tierra! Tierra!" Changing course to align his ships with this overhead harbinger of salvation, he avoided being drawn into the northern-flowing Gulf Stream, which was waiting to be charted by Ben Franklin around the time our eagle became America as art. And so, on October 11 Columbus encountered the salubrious southern end of San Salvador. Instead of somewhere in the future New England, he came up the lee of the island's west coast to an easy and safe anchorage.

Lacking maps of the beachfront property before his eyes, he assumed himself in Asia because in his imagination there were only three parts to the known world: Europe, Asia, and Africa. To the day he died, Columbus doubted he had come upon a fourth part even though Europeans had already begun appropriating through the agency of maps what to them was a New World, a new continent. Perhaps the greatest visual statement of the general confusion that rocked the Old World as word spread of Columbus's interrupted journey to Asia is the Ruysch map of 1507 (see page viii). Here we see our nascent home inserted into the template created in the second century by Ptolemy, a mathematician, astrologer, and geographer of the Greco-Roman known world, the *oikoumene.*

This map changed my life. It opened my eyes to the power of a true cultural landscape. It taught me that I must always *look* at what I *see* on a map, focusing my attention on why the map was made, not who made it, when or where it was made, but *why.* The Ruysch map was made to circulate the current news. It is a quiet meditative moment in a very busy, noisy time. It is life on the cusp of a new order. And the new order is what Henry Steele Commager christened the "utopian romance" that is America. No longer were maps merely mirrors of nature for me. No longer were the old ones "incorrect" and ignorant of the "truth." No longer did they exist simply to orient me in the practical world. The Ruysch map is reality circa 1507! It is a time machine. It makes the invisible past visible. Blessedly free of impossible abstractions and idealized virtues, it is undeniably my sort of primary historical document.

The same year, 1507, the Waldseemüller map appeared (see page ix). It is yet another reality and one very close to the one we hold dear. There we Americans are named for the first time. And there we sit, an independent continent with oceans on both sides of us, six years *before* Balboa supposedly

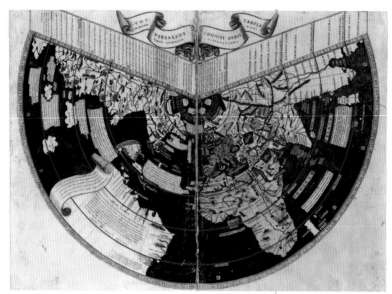

Ruysch map, 1507

person and a person who can think in pictures. This is the modus operandi of a mapmaker recording the world in images for the visually literate. For a traditional historian, maps are merely archival devices dealing with scientific accuracy. They cannot "see" a map as a first-person, visual narrative crammed with very particular insights to the process of social history. However, the true nature of maps as a key player in the history of the human imagination is a cornerstone of our series.

The very title of this volume, *Illinois: Mapping the Prairie State through History*, makes it clear that this series has a specific agenda, as does each map. It aims to thrust us all into a new intimacy with the American experience by detailing the creative process of our nation in motion through time and space via word *and* image. It grows from the relatively recent shift in consciousness about the physical, mental, and spiritual relevance of maps in our understanding of our lives on Earth. Just as each state is an integral part of the larger United States, "Where are we?" is a piece of the larger puzzle called "Who are we?"

The Library of Congress was founded in 1800 with 740 volumes and three maps. It has grown into the world's largest library and is known as "America's Memory." For me, its vast visual holdings made by those who helped build this nation make the Library the eyes of our nation as well. There are nearly five million maps

discovered "the other sea." There are few maps as mysterious for cartographic scholars as Waldseemüller's masterpiece. Where did all that news come from? For our purposes it is sufficient to say to the world's visual imagination, "Welcome to us Americans in all our cartographic splendor!"

Throughout my academic life, maps were never offered to me as primary historical documents. When I became a picture editor, I learned, to my amazement, that most book editors are logocentric, or "word people." (And thank God! If they weren't, I wouldn't have my career.) Along with most historians and academics, they make their livelihood working with words and ideas. The fact of my being an "author" makes me a word person, too, of course.

But I store information visually, as does a map. (If I ask myself where my keys are, I "see" them in my mind's eye; I don't inform myself of their whereabouts in words.) So I, like everyone who reveres maps as storytellers, am both a word

Waldseemüller map, 1507

in the Geography and Map Division. We have linked our series with that great collection in the hopes that its astonishing breadth will inspire us in our efforts to strike Lincoln's "mystic chords of memory" and create living history.

On January 25, 1786, Thomas Jefferson wrote to Archibald Stuart, "Our confederacy must be viewed as the nest from which all America, North and South, is to be peopled." This is a man who could not live without books. This is a man who drew maps. This is a politician who in spite of his abhorrence of slavery and his respect for Native Americans took pragmatic rather than principled positions when confronted by both "issues." Nonetheless, his bold vision of an expanded American universe informs our current enterprise. There is no denying that the story of the United States has a dark side. What makes the American narrative unique is the ability

we have displayed time and again to remedy our mistakes, to adjust to changing circumstances, to debate, and then move on in new directions that seem better for all.

For Jefferson, whose library was the basis for the current Library of Congress after the British burned the first one during the War of 1812, and for his contemporaries, the doctrine of progress was a keystone of the Enlightenment. The maps in our books are reports on America, and all of their political programs are manifestations of progress. Our starting fresh, free of Old World hierarchies, class attitudes, and the errors of tradition, is wedded to our geographical isolation and its immunity from the endless internal European wars devastating humanity, which justify Jefferson's confessing, "I like the dreams of the future better than the history of the past." But, as the historian Michael Kammen explains, "For much of our history we have been present-minded; yet a usable past has been needed to give shape and substance to national identity." Historical maps keep the past warm with life and immediately around us. They encourage critical inquiry, curiosity, and qualms.

For me, this series of books celebrating each of our states is not about the delineation of property rights. It is a depiction of the pursuit of happiness, which is listed as one of our natural rights in the 1776 Declaration of Independence. (Thirteen years later, when the French revolutionaries drafted a Declaration of the Rights of Man, they included "property rights," and Jefferson unsuccessfully urged them to substitute "pursuit of happiness" for "property.") Jefferson also believed, "The Earth belongs always to the living generation." I believe these books depict what each succeeding generation in its pursuit of happiness accomplished on this portion of the Earth known as the United States. If America is a matter of an idea, then maps are an image of that idea.

I also fervently believe these books will show the states linked in the same way Lincoln saw the statement that all men are created equal as "the electric cord in that Declaration that links the hearts of patriotic and liberty-loving men together, that will link those patriotic hearts as long as the love of freedom exists in the minds of men throughout the world."

VINCENT VIRGA
WASHINGTON, D.C.
2010

Introduction

The geography of Illinois was shaped over a period of centuries. Glaciers leveled most of the state, but bypassed some sections. Although people tend to think of Illinois as relentlessly flat, the state actually offers a variety of landscapes, including forested hills, ravines, river bluffs, woods, and prairies. Many Illinois locations are historically significant, and a tour of the state can be rewarding from numerous perspectives.

Illinois is a long state, nearly 380 miles from north to south. The city of Waukegan (near the Wisconsin line) is farther north than Windsor, Ontario, in Canada. At the other end of the spectrum, Cairo, Illinois, is forty miles farther south than Richmond, Virginia.

In the northeast region of the state, the terrain is dotted with small hills, lakes, and marshes. When the glaciers of the last Ice Age moved through the area, they left long, expansive ridges with irregular crests called *moraines.* An example of this landscape can be seen in Moraine Hills State Park near McHenry (McHenry County). Lake Defiance, in the center of the park, was formed when a large chunk of ice broke away from the main glacier and melted. Human habitation of the park area dates back to around 4000 B.C.

The crown jewel of the northeast region—and indeed the state as a whole—is Chicago (Cook County), one of the nation's most powerful industrial and cultural centers. Chicago occupies a low stretch of land along Lake Michigan, which once covered the entire area. From a historical perspective, the Chicago Loop area alone offers countless places and happenings worthy of exploration. Approximately 74 percent of the population of Illinois resides in the northeastern corner of the state, primarily within the city of Chicago and the surrounding area.

Starved Rock State Park near Utica (LaSalle County) is located in north-central Illinois. A remarkable pedestal of sandstone, The Rock—or Le Rocher in French—was the site of Fort St. Louis, constructed by René-Robert Cavelier, Sieur de La Salle in 1682. The name "Starved Rock" comes from a legend that tells of a band of Illiniwek Indians starving to death on the rock while under siege by the Potawatomi and Ottawa.

The northwest region of Illinois escaped glaciation in the last glacial period. The deepest valleys and tallest hills in Illinois can be found here, including Charles Mound (Jo Daviess County), the highest point in the state at 1,235 feet above sea level. The area is known for unusual and beautiful rock formations, breathtaking canyons, wooded ravines, waterfalls, and lofty, steep cliffs. Cities in the northwest region include Peoria (Peoria County), one of the oldest settlements in Illinois.

Those who think the central section of the state is one big corn field will be surprised to discover Sand Ridge State Forest in west-central Illinois. The requisite open fields and grasslands are there, but the area also contains wooded ridges created from one-hundred-foot-high sand dunes. During a prehistoric dry period, shifting winds sculpted the dunes out of a vast deposit of sand left by a receding glacier. Prickly pear cactus and coyotes give Sand Ridge State Forest a "southwestern" feel.

The largest city in the central region is Springfield (Sangamon County), the capital of Illinois. The spirit of Abraham Lincoln is alive and well in Springfield, where visitors can explore Lincoln's home and tomb, as well as the nearby New Salem Historic Site, where Lincoln spent his early adulthood.

In Douglas, Moultrie, and Coles Counties approximately 4,500 members of the Amish faith maintain a community with its own unique history and culture. The first Amish families settled in central Illinois in 1865.

The southwest section of the state is characterized by rich farmlands as well as limestone bluffs. Located just outside Collinsville (Madison County) is the Cahokia Mounds State Historic Site. This site contains the remains of an ancient city founded by a Mississippian people that flourished from A.D. 700 to 1400, then disappeared. At the center of the historical site is Monks Mound, the largest prehistoric earthen mound in North America.

Illinois offers yet another landscape variation in the southeastern part of the state. Stretching for seventy miles, east to west, the Illinois Ozarks extend from Grand Tower on the Mississippi River to Shawneetown on the Ohio. The area features a stunning combination of high canyon walls, shady gorges, sandstone cliff faces, and dense forest canopy. Southern Illinois also encompasses the Cache River Wetlands near Belknap (Johnson County). This is swamp country—home of massive cypress trees and myriad amphibians, reptiles, birds, insects, and mammals.

Tunnel Hill State Trail near Vienna (Johnson County) takes hikers along the route of the Vincennes and Cairo Railroad founded by Civil War general Ambrose Burnside. Standing in the narrow tunnel, it's easy to imagine the rumble of the cars along the tracks.

The southern region of Illinois is also perfect for growing grapes. The Shawnee Hills Wine Trail takes tourists to a dozen wineries in Jackson and Union Counties.

In addition to its varied landscape, Illinois boasts an enormously diverse population with roots in a multitude of countries. The French started it all in 1673, but failed to significantly colonize the area. In the end, American frontiersmen from a wide range of backgrounds made Illinois their own. The first Europeans to settle in southern Illinois moved into the area from Kentucky and Tennessee in the early 1800s. They had little in common with the New Englanders who settled the northern part of the state. Differences in ancestry, religious beliefs, and lifestyle were never more evident than during the Civil War. The cliffs and canyons of southern Illinois harbored both Union and Confederate soldiers.

As the largest city in Illinois, Chicago has always been a magnet for people of all nationalities. In 1870 more than half its residents were foreign-born. They came overwhelmingly from Europe, with Germans the largest single group. By 1990 metropolitan Chicago had more residents born in Latin America than Europe, almost as many from Asia, and thousands from Africa and the Caribbean. Mexicans formed the largest single group.

The earliest settlers in Rockford (Winnebago County) were from New York and New England. The Irish arrived in the early 1850s, followed by the Swedes. Other ethnic groups also appeared, including Italians, Poles, and Lithuanians, and more recently Laotians, Vietnamese, and Hispanics.

Illinois place names reflect the diverse backgrounds of those who have called the area home. Many county and city names honor Native American tribes, for example, Cahokia, Havana, Kickapoo, Maroa (a contraction of Tamaroa, one of the tribes of the Illinois confederacy), Peoria, and Winnebago. A number of place names are believed to have come directly from names given by Native Americans to the place in question. Examples include Chicago, Kankakee, Kishwaukee, Nippersink, Pecatonica, Sinnissippi, Shokokon, Somonauk, and Maquon.

The French legacy is carried on through many place names, including Belleville ("beautiful city"), Bourbonnais (named after fur trapper François Bourbonnais), Creve Coeur ("heartbreak"), Du Quoin (named for Jean Baptiste Du Quoin, son of a Frenchman and a Tamaroa Indian woman), Moline (from the French word *moulin,* meaning mill), Prairie du Rocher ("prairie of the rock"), and Wilmette (named for French-Canadian Antoine Ouilmette). The city of Joliet used to be called Juliet, which may have been a reference to Shakespeare's play (Romeoville is about ten miles north). In 1845 local residents changed the community's name permanently from "Juliet" to "Joliet," in honor of the French explorer Louis Jolliet.

In the early nineteenth century Schaumburg was founded by German settlers, many of whom came from a region of Germany called Schaumburg-Lippe. Germans tended to bring place names with them, as evidenced by the fact that there have been multiple Hanovers, Berlins, Hamburgs, and Bremens in Illinois. Dutch farmers founded South Holland in the 1840s. Swedish religious dissidents settled Bishop Hill (Biskopskulla in Swedish) in 1846.

The chapters in this book take the reader from the first encounters between Native Americans and Europeans through territorial transitions, wars, and enormous economic changes, while highlighting the Prairie State's varied geography, colorful history, and diverse cultural heritage. The maps in this book expand and enrich our understanding of when, how, and why Illinois became the remarkable place it is today.

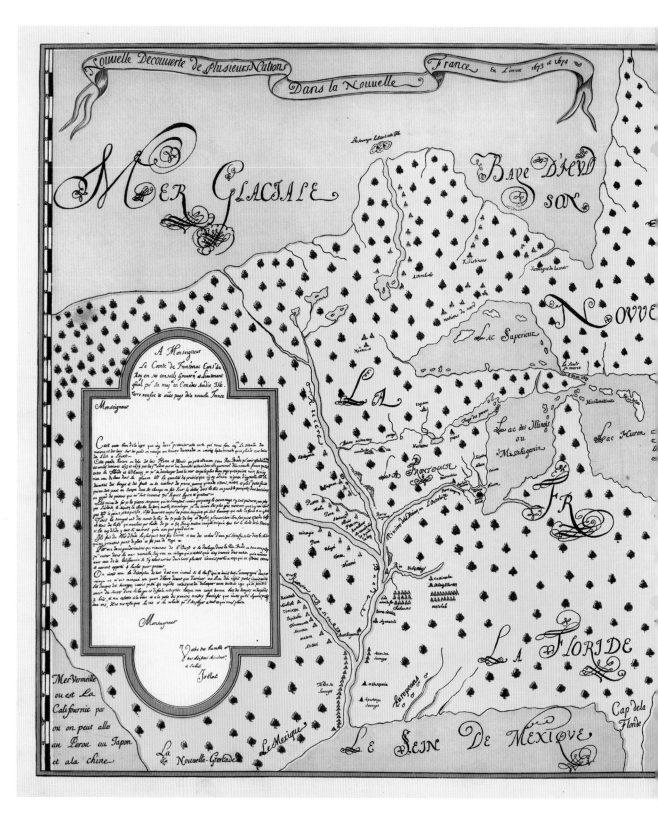

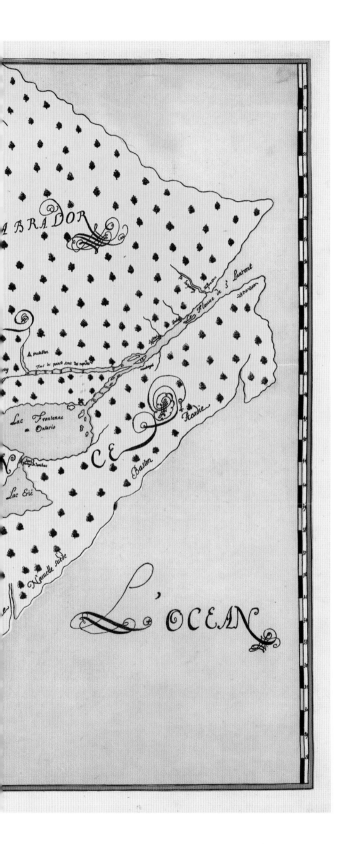

Nouvelle decouverte de plusieurs nations
dans la Nouvelle France—Joliet (1673 or 1674)

This map, drawn by French-Canadian fur trapper and explorer Louis Jolliet (sometimes spelled Joliet), depicts North America. In addition to showing the Great Lakes, St. Lawrence and Mississippi Rivers, and the northwest coast (as part of the Glacial Sea), it includes locations of Native American villages. Note that Lake Michigan is labeled "Lac des Illinois"—Lake of the Illinois (Indians). The map is dedicated to Louis de Baude Frontenac, royally appointed governor of New France.

*Carte de la decouverte faite l'an
1673 dans l'Amerique Septentrionale
—Marquette*

Oriented with north to the right, this
map was probably the first printed map
to show the full length of the Mississippi
River. Green Bay would be at the bottom
right and New Orleans at the upper left.
The locations of Native American villages are also shown. One of the most
intriguing labels on the map is "Nations
qui ont des chevaux et des chameaux"
(nations who have horses and camels).
The "camels" were most likely bison. This
map accompanied Father Jacques Marquette's report on his 1673 Mississippi
River voyage, published in 1681.

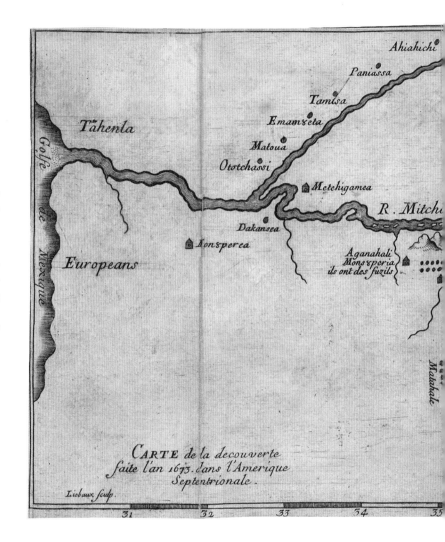

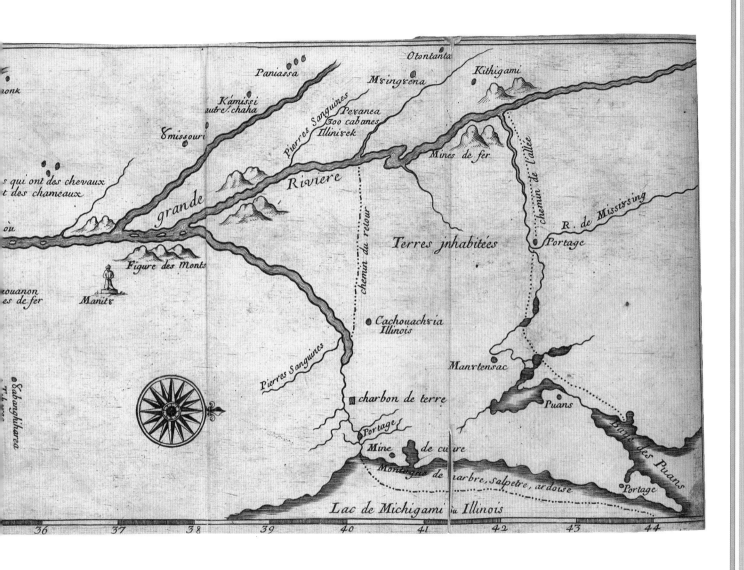

Otontanta

Paniassa

Mingsena

Kithigami

Kamissi
autre I. chaha

Pesanea
300 cabanes
Illinisek

Pierres Sanguines

Smissouri

Mines de fer

s qui ont des chevaux
t des chameaux

grande

Riviere

R. de Missirsing

Terres jnhabitées

chemin de l'allée

Portage

Figure des Monts

ou

rouanon
es de fer

Manits

chemin du retour

Cachouachsia
Illinois

Sabaughkarea

Pierres Sanguines

Manrtensac

Puans

charbon de terre

Baue des Puans

Portage

Mine   de cuivre

Montagne de marbre, salpetre, ardoise

Portage

Lac de Michigami ou Illinois

36   37   38   39   40   41   42   43   44

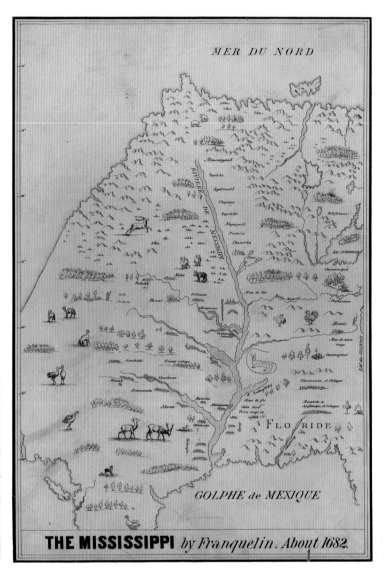

The Mississippi—Franquelin (ca. 1682)

Royal hydrographer Jean Baptiste Louis Franquelin probably copied and compiled this map from material provided by Louis Jolliet. Published around 1682, this particular map depicts the whole course of the Mississippi in much the same manner as the map that accompanied Marquette's report in 1681. However, on the Franquelin map, the Mississippi is indistinctly prolonged to the north, and the coasts of the Northern Ocean ("Mer du Nord") are near its head. The map also features trees, animals, and names of Indian nations. Franquelin's drawings of "camels" (also mentioned by Marquette) resemble Bactrian camels. However, historians believe that the animals Marquette called camels were actually bison.

First Encounters

Archaeologists believe that the earliest inhabitants of North America arrived during the Stone Age by crossing a land bridge between Siberia and Alaska. At that time, glaciers covered much of North America, including the area now known as the Midwestern United States.

As these glaciers receded, descendants of the original immigrants from Asia made their way south, probably arriving in Illinois between 10,000 and 8000 B.C. These Paleo-Indians typically lived in small camps in forests, where they subsisted on large game and wild plants. By 1000 B.C., a lot had changed. The area boasted numerous villages—most erected near waterways—and far-ranging trade networks.

Around A.D. 700, members of what archaeologists call the Middle Mississippian culture built a massive community near present-day Cahokia, Illinois. Covering six square miles, the city of Cahokia was inhabited by ten thousand to twenty thousand people. Over time, this highly developed civilization built more than one hundred earthen mounds. One of these—Monks Mound—is the largest ancient earthwork in North America. For reasons not clearly understood, the Middle Mississippian culture began to decline around the 1200s. By A.D. 1400 the site at Cahokia had been abandoned.

Early in the sixteenth century, a loose confederation of Algonquian-speaking Indians migrated from southern Michigan into northern Illinois and southern Wisconsin. Today, we commonly refer to this tribe as the Illinois or Illiniwek, sometimes shortened to Illini. Linguists believe the tribe called itself "inoca." Studies suggest that Ojibwa Indians heard the Illinois use the word "irenweewa"—meaning "he speaks in an ordinary way"—and began calling the tribe "ilinwe" (plural: "ilinwek"). French explorers gave "ilinwe" a French spelling, rendering it "Ilinois" or "Illinois."

The Illinois tribe consisted of about a dozen separate bands, including the Cahokia, Kaskaskia, Michigamea, Moingwena, Peoria, and Tamaroa. Their total population was around eight thousand in the early 1500s. A typical year for the Illinois included planting and harvesting crops, hunting buffalo and other game, and attacking other tribes and taking prisoners. Depending on the time of year, they lived either in villages consisting of substantial rectangular cabins or in pole-framed shelters covered by mats made of flat rushes.

During the first half of the seventeenth century, the Iroquois Confederacy (headquartered in New York and Pennsylvania) expanded its empire westward. As a result, the Huron, Sauk, Fox, Potawatomi, Kickapoo, Shawnee, and Miami tribes were pushed into Illinois territory. This created a fair amount of trouble, but the crushing blow came when the Iroquois themselves arrived in Illinois, forcing the Illinois Indians—who now numbered roughly thirteen thousand—to flee the area. The Iroquois Wars ended in 1701 with a declaration of peace by the Iroquois.

By that time, French exploration of Illinois was under way. Representatives of the French government had claimed ownership of Illinois and adjacent lands in 1671, and in 1673 the first official French expedition into Illinois set out from St. Ignace (located in present-day Michigan). Leading that expedition were Louis Jolliet, a twenty-seven-year-old Canadian fur trader and mapmaker, and Father Jacques Marquette, a thirty-five-year-old Jesuit priest. Jolliet's primary goal was to find the great river the Indians called "Misi Sipi." The river was believed to lead to the Pacific Ocean, and would be invaluable to the French in their effort to sustain their fur trade monopoly. Marquette's mission was to convert the Illinois Indians to Christianity.

Jolliet, Marquette, and the other five members of the expedition left St. Ignace on May 17, 1673, in two canoes. They traveled along Lake Michigan to Green Bay, Wisconsin. Aided by Miami Indians, they journeyed south via the Fox River and Wisconsin River. By June 17 they were on the Mississippi River. About a week later they arrived at a village inhabited by members of the Peoria band of the Illinois Indians.

After spending a few days with the Peoria, Jolliet and his party traveled down the Mississippi, encountering another Illinois tribe, the Michigamea. Not many days after that, the members of the expedition determined that the Mississippi River did not lead to the Pacific Ocean. Unwilling to risk encounters with hostile Indians or the Spanish, the explorers headed back toward Canada.

Their route up the Illinois River brought them into contact with a band of Kaskaskia Indians (also part of the Illinois "family"). Marquette promised to return to the village to establish a mission. Illness forced him to remain at Green Bay while the others continued up into Canada. On the outskirts of Montreal, Jolliet's canoe capsized. Two men riding with him perished, and Jolliet's maps and records of the journey were lost. Jolliet had to re-create them from memory.

In 1675 Marquette returned to the Kaskaskia Indians and established a mission near present-day Utica. He became ill again, and died on his way back to St. Ignace.

The next explorer of note to venture into Illinois country was René Robert Cavelier, Sieur de La Salle. Accompanied by Henri de Tonti, an Italian soldier of fortune, La Salle took an expedition into the area in 1680. On that trip, Fort Crèvecoeur was built on the future site of Peoria, Illinois. Financial problems forced La Salle to return to Canada. He came back to Illinois a few months later, only to find that the men stationed at Fort Crèvecoeur had mutinied. The fort was in ruins. Not only that, the Iroquois had destroyed the Kaskaskia mission site, and Tonti had been severely wounded.

Tonti recovered and traveled with La Salle and his party down the Mississippi River to the

Gulf of Mexico. On behalf of France, La Salle claimed all the lands touched by all the rivers that flowed into the Mississippi River. He named the tract Louisiana after King Louis XIV.

On their way back to Canada, La Salle and Tonti built Fort St. Louis on a promontory known as Starved Rock in Illinois. According to legend, a band of Illinois Indians had starved to death at that location while under siege by the Potawatomi and allied Ottawa.

La Salle returned to France, where he asked the king for two ships and outlined his plan to invade Spanish territory with an army of Indians. In 1684 he was killed by his own men after a series of misfortunes that culminated in La Salle's boat running aground in Texas. Tonti took up the mantle and was instrumental in increasing the French presence in Illinois over the next fifteen years. He died of yellow fever in 1704.

The French continued to build villages and missions just south of where the Missouri, Illinois, and Mississippi Rivers converge, in an area that became known as the American Bottom. By the end of the seventeenth century, the Fox Indians had become so hostile that the French withdrew from northern Illinois.

For most of the eighteenth century, a village named Kaskaskia was the leading French settlement in Illinois. Founded in 1703, the town was dubbed "Paris of the West" and viewed as the cultural and commercial capital of Illinois. The villages of Prairie du Roche and Fort de Chartres were established not far from Kaskaskia.

In 1717 the French colony of Louisiana annexed the Illinois country. By the middle of the century, France's holdings included Canada, the Mississippi River, and several seaports on the Gulf of Mexico.

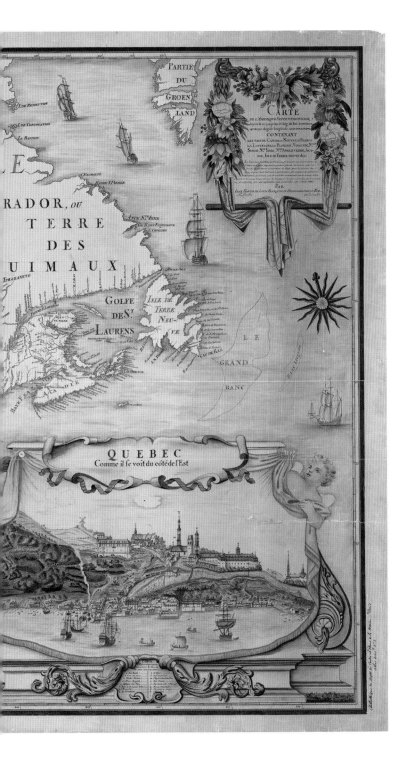

*Carte de l'Amerique Septentrionnale:
depuis le 25, jusqu'au 65⁰ deg. de latt. &
environ 140, & 235 deg. de longitude—
Franquelin (1688)*

This map of North America, published in 1909 or 1910, was copied by official court cartographer Jean Baptiste Louis Franquelin from the original 1688 manuscript. The map shows the Mississippi, Illinois, and Ohio Rivers as well as Fort St. Louis, built by French explorer René-Robert Cavelier, Sieur de La Salle in 1682 near present-day Utica, Illinois, in La Salle County. The site is now known as Starved Rock. Also labeled is "Fort Checagou," a French military fortification in the Chicago area, the existence of which has never been proven. It is possible that it was simply a small fortified French trading post.

Carte de la riviere Longue, et de quelques autres, qui se dechargent dans le grand fleuve de Missisipi [sic] ... ; Carte que les Gnacsitares ont dessine sur des paux de cerfs—Lahontan (1703)

The map on the left side of this page covers the area west of the Minnesota River. Its title in English is: "A Map drawn upon stag skins by the Gnacsitares." The map on the right side covers the Minnesota River, Lake Superior, Lake Michigan, and the Mississippi River south to Saint Louis. Its title in English is: "A Map of the Long River and of some others that fall into that final part of the Great River of Mississippi which is here laid down." A number of early French forts and fur trading outposts appear on the map. Insets include: "The dwelling houses of the Tahuglauk," "The Vessels used by the Tahuglauk," and "A medal of the Tahuglauk." Historians have long believed that the Long River—depicted as flowing from the western mountains (Rocky Mountains) and connecting to the Mississippi River—existed only in the imagination of mapmaker Baron de Lahontan, along with the "Tahuglauk" and "Gnacsitares" Indian tribes whose houses, boats, and medals he sketched on the map.

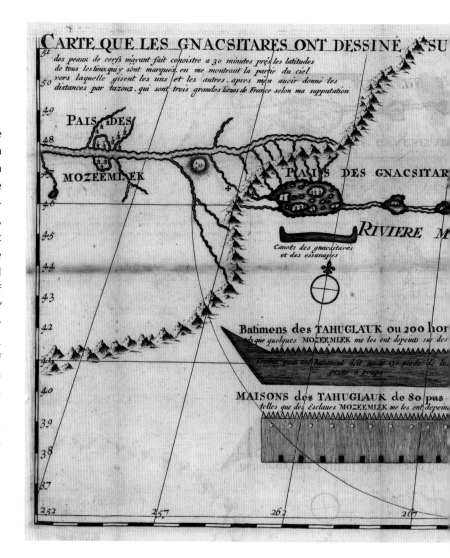

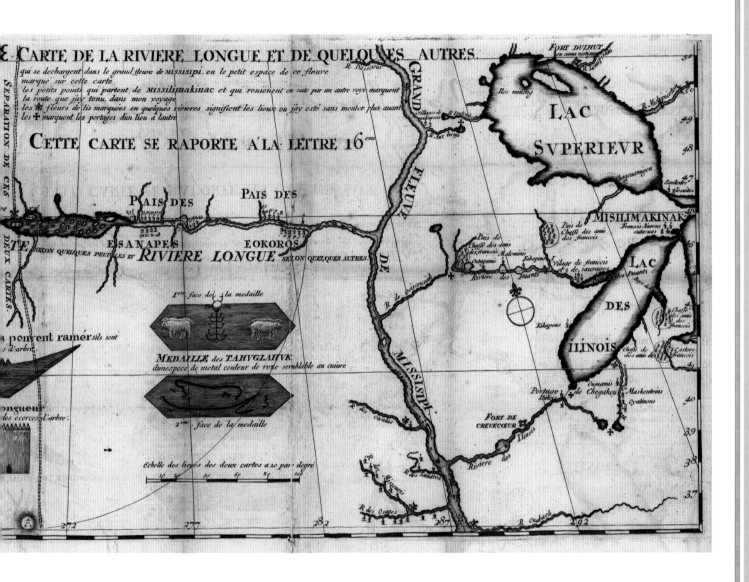

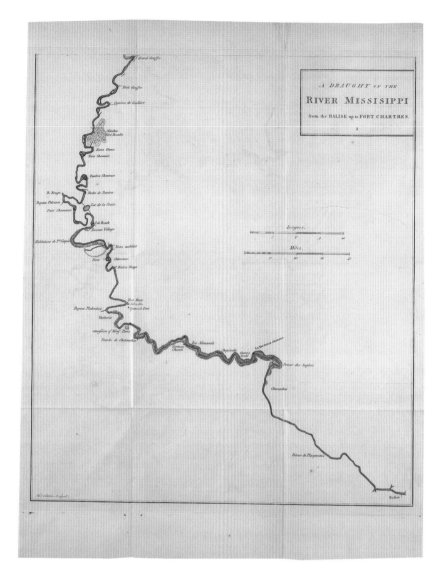
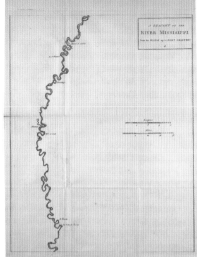
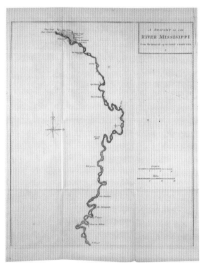

A draught of the Missisippi [sic] River from Balise up to Fort Chartres—Pittman (1770)

Printed in 1770, these maps were created by Captain Philip Pittman of the Royal British engineers. Pittman included the maps in his book, *The Present State of the European Settlements on the Mississippi,* a record of his experiences and observations while he was surveying the area in the 1760s. The starting point (in the lower right corner of the first section of the map) is Fort Balise, located at the eastern mouth of the Mississippi River. At the top of the third section of the map is Fort Chartres, a French military fortification built in 1720. The village of Prairie du Rocher—located fifty miles south of St. Louis, Missouri, in present-day Randolph County, Illinois—was established near the fort in 1722.

Early Illinois: Territorial Transitions

FROM THE LATE 1600S TO THE MIDDLE OF THE 1700s, Illinois was primarily under the control of the French—at least according to the French. In 1671 representatives of the French government claimed ownership of Illinois and adjacent lands, much to the bewilderment of Native American tribes who witnessed the ceremony.

In 1749 King George II of England presented a group of British investors with land in the Ohio Valley. In response to the objections of France, the British declared that John Cabot had claimed all of North America for England during the fifteenth century. Something had to give.

Between 1754 and 1760 the British battled the French for control of the New World. Although American Indians fought on both sides, the name given to the conflict—the French and Indian War—reflects the strong Indian allegiance to the French. In 1763 the Illinois country was ceded to Britain by the Treaty of Paris. Before long, French influence remained only in place names such as Joliet, Le Roy, Bourbonnais, Marseilles, and—of course—Illinois.

In an effort to ease relations with the American Indians, King George III issued a proclamation prohibiting settlement west of the Appalachian Mountains and requiring those already living in those regions to return east. Settlers ignored the edict. It soon became apparent that resistance to that particular proclamation was the least of King George's worries.

Tensions between the colonies and the Mother Country rose at an alarming rate. On March 23, 1775, in Virginia, Patrick Henry delivered his famous speech against British rule, in which he declared: "Give me liberty or give me death!"

In Illinois the American Revolution brought attacks on colonial settlements by Indians allied with the British. Virginia native George Rogers Clark, an explorer and soldier, was instrumental in planning and executing the conquest of the Illinois country on behalf of Virginia. Thanks to his defeat of the British at Kaskaskia in 1778, Illinois became a county of the Old Dominion. At this time, Illinois was home to a wide variety of ethnic cultures, including Indian, Spanish, British, French, and American.

A subsequent Treaty of Paris, this one signed in 1783, extended the boundaries of the United States to include the Illinois country, formally ending any British claim to the area. Virginia ceded its claim in 1784, leaving no one officially in charge of the Illinois country. Chaos reigned. Settlers felt abandoned and helpless. The Indians wanted all whites to evacuate the area and expressed that preference in no uncertain terms.

In 1787 Congress passed the Northwest Ordinance, organizing the Northwest Territory, which included the Illinois country. In 1788 Arthur St. Clair, a Revolutionary War hero, was appointed governor of the territory. Clashes between white Americans and Indians, who continued to receive British support, persisted after St. Clair became governor. When peace negotiations failed, General "Mad Anthony" Wayne and his troops arrived on the scene. In 1794 Wayne routed a confederacy of eight Indian tribes led by Blue Jacket, a Shawnee, at the Battle of Fallen Timbers in Ohio. The resulting Treaty of Greenville established a new Indian boundary line and gave Americans control of much of the Northwest Territory.

A law passed in 1800 divided the Northwest Territory into two parts: the Indiana Territory (consisting of Illinois, Indiana, Wisconsin, Minnesota, and part of Michigan) and the Northwest Territory (consisting of Ohio and part of Michigan). At that time, the population of Illinois was roughly 2,500, not many more than the number reported fifty years earlier. Parts of Illinois were virtually uninhabited by whites. Reasons included harsh conditions, Indian raids, a lack of effective government, delays in the opening of land for sale, and a huge mosquito population that raised the threat of malaria.

The paucity of trees made it difficult to build houses and barns. It was believed that a key sign of rich soil was the presence of tall trees, and these were notably scarce in the prairie landscape. Once farmers realized that Illinois soil was rich and fertile, more pioneers made their way into the area. In 1809 the Illinois Territory was created, with Kaskaskia as its capital and Ninian Edwards as governor. Farming was the primary occupation. Commercial coal mining began in Illinois around 1810.

Tensions mounted again between Indians and whites. In 1811 an army led by William Henry Harrison defeated Tecumseh's Native-American Confederation at the Battle of Tippecanoe in Indiana. About nine months later, Potawatomi warriors ambushed a group of soldiers, women, and children on their way from Fort Dearborn (in what is now Chicago) to Fort Wayne (Indiana). By this time, the United States was at war with Great Britain and its Indian allies.

Neither the Americans nor the British won a clear victory in the War of 1812, but the native peoples of North America were undoubtedly the losers. They could no longer count on support from the British, and successive treaties caused them to vanish from the Illinois Territory within two decades.

Illinois became the twenty-first state in 1818. Kaskaskia was chosen as the state capital, and Shadrach Bond was inaugurated as the first governor. In subsequent years, new towns were laid out, newspapers were founded, and schools and prisons were built. Transportation to the East Coast improved with the completion of the Erie Canal.

During this time, a culture clash developed in the state. Northern and central Illinois were occupied largely by "Yankees"—people who had come from the northeastern and mid-Atlantic states. In the southern part of the state, inhabitants were more likely to be "Southerners" or "Plain Folks," as they were sometimes called, who hailed from Kentucky or Tennessee. There were significant differences between these two groups in terms of their reasons for settling in Illinois, their religious beliefs, and lifestyles. Even their dietary habits were different. By the middle of the century, these disparities were demonstrated on a larger scale as divisions between North and South at a national level became more pronounced and disturbing.

For the time being, however, advances in transportation and trade took center stage. Thanks to steamboats and the railroads, Chicago emerged as a major transportation hub. In 1836 the Galena and Chicago railroad was chartered and construction was finished on the Illinois and Michigan Canal connecting Lake Michigan with the Illinois River. The Illinois Central rail line was completed between Chicago, Galena, and Cairo in 1856, the same year that Chicago's Union Stock Yards opened.

In 1857 Illinois State Normal University was founded as the first public institution of higher education in the state. At this point, the population of Illinois was roughly 851,500. In Springfield, the new state capital, a young man named Abraham Lincoln was enlarging the house he shared with his wife, Mary Todd, to accommodate a growing family.

At Springfield on June 16, 1858, Lincoln was nominated by the Republicans as a candidate for the United States Senate. In accepting the nomination, he delivered his House Divided Speech, which included these radical, forceful, and prophetic words: "I believe this government cannot endure, permanently half slave and half free. . . . It will become all one thing or all the other."

PARTIE OCCIDENTALE
DE LA VIRGINIE, PENSYLVANIE
MARYLAND ET CAROLINE SEPT.LE
la Riviere d'Ohio, et toutes celles qui s'y jettent
partie de la Riviere MISSISSIPI
tout le Cours de la Riviere des Illinois
LE LAC ERIE, PARTIE DES LACS HURON,
ET MICHIGAN &.
Toutes les Contrées qui Bordent
ces Lacs et Rivieres
Par Hutchins Capitaine Anglais
A PARIS
Chez le Rouge Rue des grands Augustins
1781

Partie occidentale de la Virginie, Pensylvanie, Maryland, et Caroline Septle;
la rivière d'Ohio, et toutes celles qui s'y jettent, partie de la Rivière Mississippi,
tout le cours de la rivière de Illinois, le Lac Erie, partie des Lacs Huron
et Michigan &. toutes les contrées qui bordent ces lacs et rivières, par Hutchins,
capitaine anglais—Le Rouge (1781)

Originally drawn by American surveyor and mapmaker Thomas Hutchins, this western territories map was translated into French and reproduced by Paris-based map publisher Georges-Louis LeRouge in 1781. The map depicts the Ohio River Valley as it appeared in the 1700s, including the Mississippi, Illinois, Wabash, and Ohio Rivers, as well as Lakes Michigan, Erie, and Huron. Notice the section labeled Contrée des Illinois (Land of the Illinois), in the middle of which lies a "grande prairie naturelle" (vast natural grassland).

A

MAP

of the

UNITED STATES

—— *of* ——

AMERICA,

As settled by the Peace of

1783.

Publish'd Dec.ʳ 1, 1783. by I. Fielding, Paternoster Row.

*A map of the United States of America, as settled
by the peace of 1783—Fielding*

The American Revolution ended in 1783. After the Treaty of Paris was signed, John Fielding published this map of the new nation. The map includes territory east of the Mississippi River and from Canada to Florida. Boundaries, forts, major settlements, Indian tribes, and routes of commerce are indicated. The area now known as Illinois was part of Virginia at this time, having been secured for the Old Dominion by the defeat of the British at Kaskaskia in 1778 by troops under the command of George Rogers Clark.

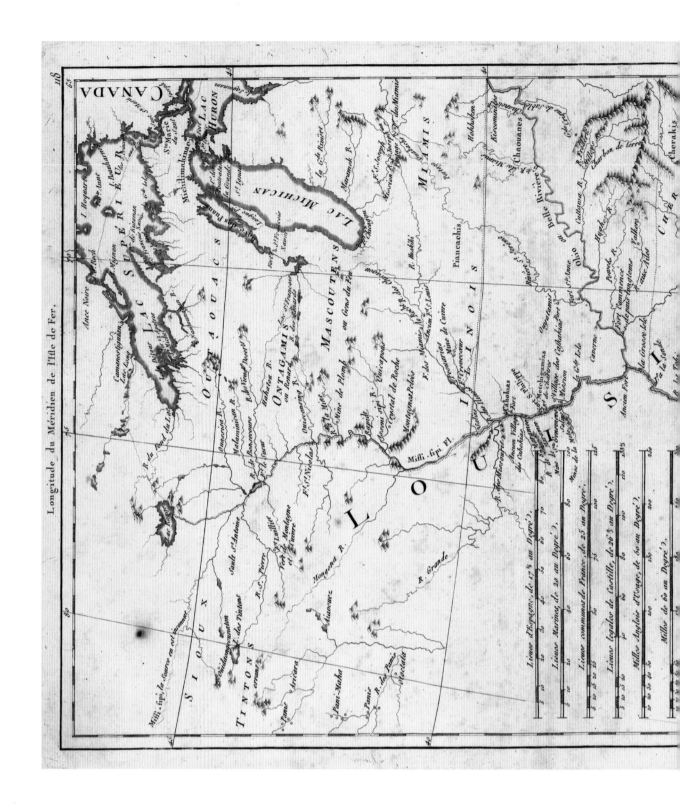

Longitude du Méridien de l'Isle de Fer.

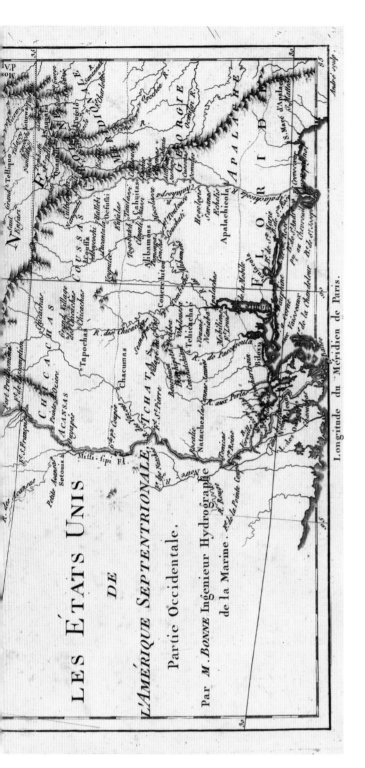

Les États Unis de l'Amérique septentrionale,
partie occidentale—Bonne (1788)

Royal cartographer Rigobert Bonne published this map of the United States five years after the end of the American Revolution. Depicting the region between the Mississippi Valley and the Appalachian Mountains in considerable detail, the map indicates the location of many French forts and Indian tribes, including the Illinois. A large mileage scale appears on the left side. The same year this map was published (1788), Arthur St. Clair, a Revolutionary War hero, was appointed governor of the Northwest Territory, of which Illinois was now a part.

North America from the Mississippi River to the Pacific,
between the 35th and 60th parallels of latitude—unknown (179-)

Probably published sometime between 1797 and 1800, this map of western North America is of unknown origin. However, the map was part of a collection belonging to William Clark and was most likely prepared for the Lewis and Clark expedition prior to 1804. Note that St. Louis is marked by an X and its name in the lower right corner. Most of the place names are in French, but Spanish origins are implied by the depiction of the Missouri River (labeled Rio Missouri), whose headwaters are erroneously shown near Santa Fe in modern-day New Mexico.

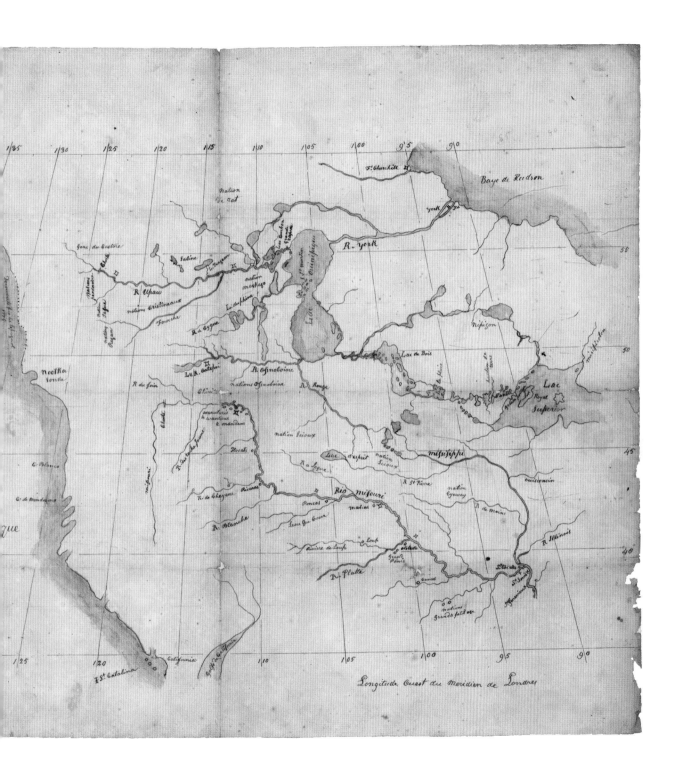

Baye de Hudson

F. Churchill

R. York

Lac Ourinipique

Nipigon

Lac du Bois

Lac Superieur

R. Asinoboine

mississippi

nation Sioux

Lac d'esprit

Rio missouri

R. Platte

California

F. St. Catalina

Nootka Sonde

R. Upau

R. Gygue

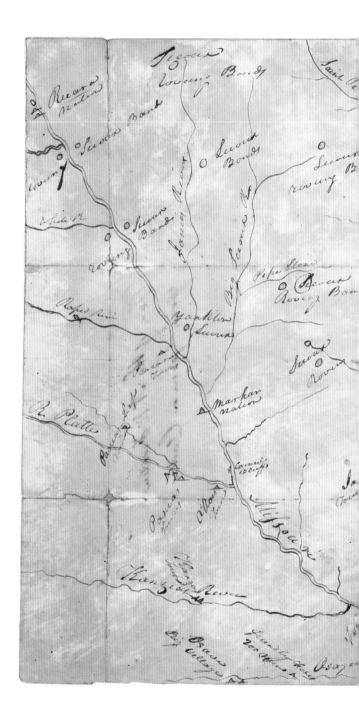

Plan of the N.W. frontier—Clarke (ca. 1813)
This map shows the Mississippi River from St. Anthony Falls (Minnesota) to St. Louis, the Missouri River west to South Dakota, the Illinois River east to Lake Michigan, and tributaries. It was created around 1813 by William Clark, an explorer, soldier, Indian agent, and governor of the Missouri Territory. Along with Meriwether Lewis, Clark explored the Northwest as the cartographer for an expedition that lasted from 1804 to 1806. Illinois locations labeled on the map include the Chicago Portage and Fort Clark (named for William Clark's brother George Rogers Clark) in Peoria County. The map also includes a list of distances to various points via riverways from Prairie du Chien and St. Louis.

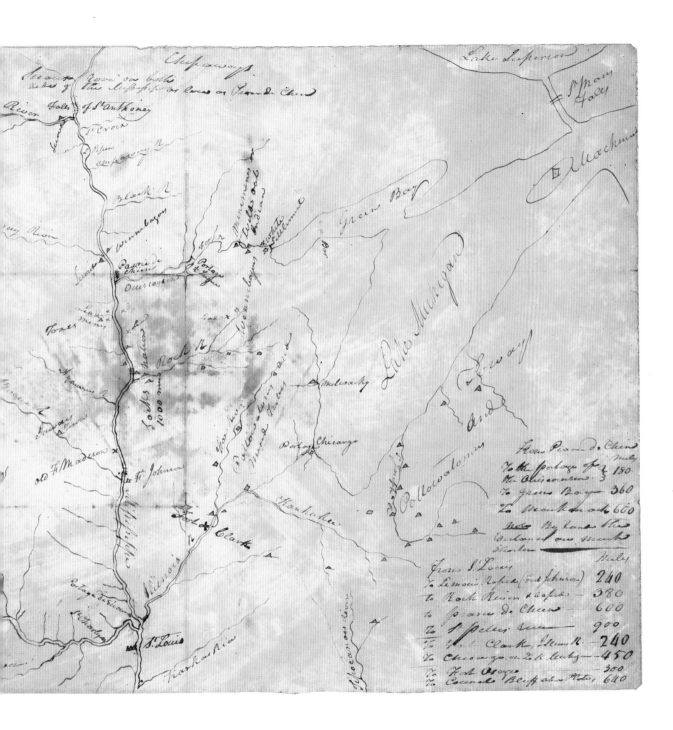

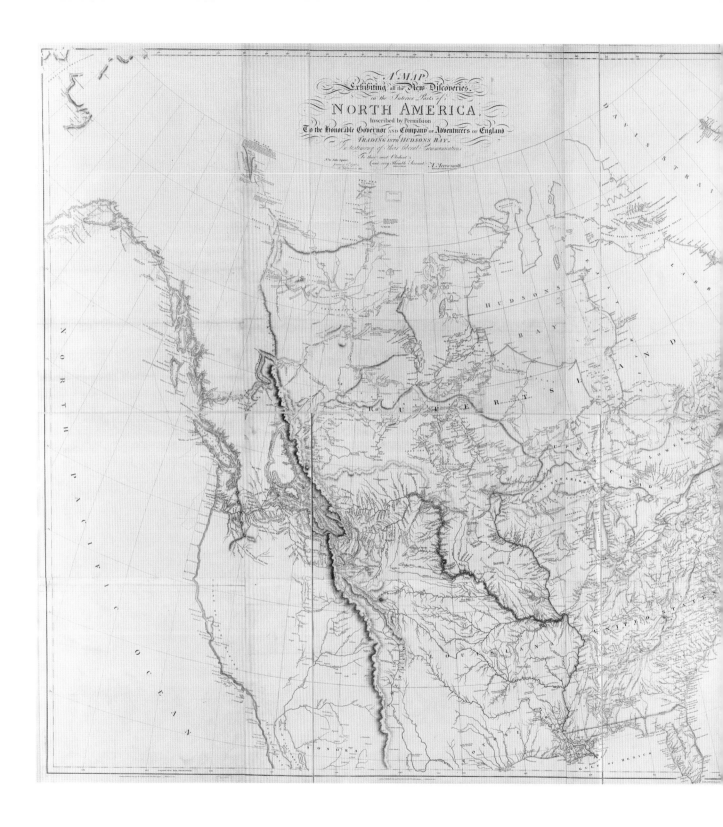

A MAP
Exhibiting all the New Discoveries
in the Interior Parts of
NORTH AMERICA
Inscribed by Permission
To the Honorable Governor and Company of Adventurers of England
TRADING INTO HUDSONS BAY
In testimony of their liberal Communications
To their most Obedient &
Very Humble Servant. A. Arrowsmith

A map exhibiting all the new discoveries in the interior parts of North America, inscribed by permission to the honorable governor and company of the adventurers of England trading into Hudsons Bay, in testimony of their liberal communications to their most obedient and very humble servant A. Arrowsmith, hydrographer to H. R. H. the Prince of Wales (January 1st 1795; revised 1814)

British surveyor Aaron Arrowsmith produced his first map of North America in 1795. His 1802 revision of that map, used in planning the Lewis and Clark Expedition, was carried by Lewis and Clark on the expedition. The map at left, an 1814 revision by Arrowsmith, incorporates the Lewis and Clark discoveries and others, showing points of interest, aids to navigation, and historical information. The label "Pootewatomis" near the tip of Lake Michigan refers to the Potawatomi tribe who, along with the Ottawas, occupied the Chicago village in 1814. It is interesting to note that St. Louis is rendered as "St. Lewis" on this map. Perhaps Arrowsmith thought the city should be named after Meriwether Lewis rather than King Louis IX of France.

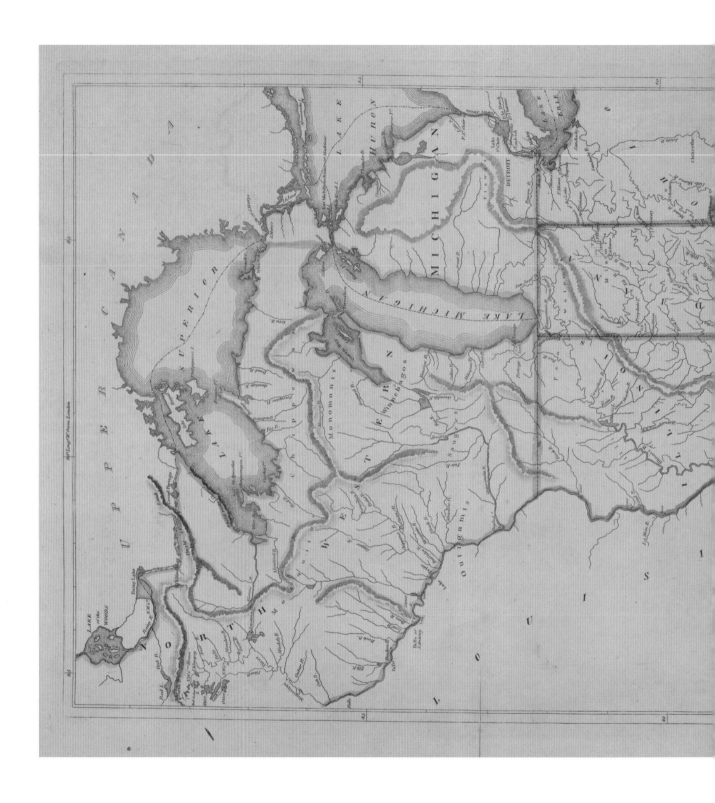

The Upper Territories of the United States—
From Carey's General Atlas (1814)

Published by Mathew Carey in 1814 and engraved by Kneass and Delleker, this map was part of the first atlas made in the United States to employ standard color on the maps. The map of the United States is an updated copy of one engraved by Henry Tanner, published in 1812. At this time, Ohio and Indiana were states; Michigan and Illinois were separate territories. Notice that the northern boundary of Illinois and Indiana has been drawn to exclude Lake Michigan, leaving Chicago outside Illinois.

Map of Illinoise [sic]—Melish (1818?)

Illinois became a state in 1818, the same year John Melish is believed to have published his Map of Illinoise [*sic*]. Born in Scotland, Melish visited the United States numerous times beginning in 1806 and eventually settled there in 1811. He was the first American publisher to issue exclusively cartographic and geographic items. Although his plan was to create a map of every state, Melish was able to complete only six before he died in 1822. The Illinois map shows settlements, military posts, township and range numbers, Kaskaskia and Shawnee Districts, roads, and boundaries of Military Bounty Lands—tracts of land given as payment to soldiers who fought in the War of 1812 against the British. In Illinois, Military Bounty Lands consisted of a triangle between the Mississippi and Illinois Rivers.

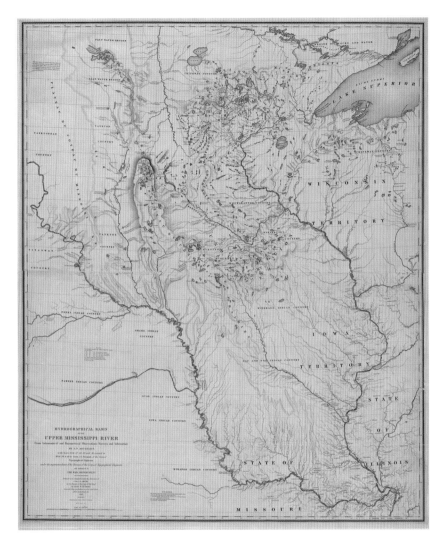

Hydrographical basin of the upper Mississippi River from astronomical and barometrical observations, surveys, and information.—J. N. Nicollet, in the years 1836, 37, 38, 39, and 40; assisted in 1838, 39 & 40, by Lieut. J. C. Fremont, of the Corps of Topographical Engineers under the superintendence of the Bureau of the Corps of Topographical Engineers and authorized by the War Department

Based on systematic instrument surveys by the French mathematician and astronomer Joseph Nicollet between 1836 and 1840, this map is the earliest accurate mapping of the interior of North America, from St. Louis north to the Canadian border and west along the Missouri River. Nicollet charted the Mississippi River using mathematical calculations to confirm the true source of the Mississippi. Published in 1843, the map shows the western portion of Illinois in the lower right corner. Numerous Illinois cities are labeled, including Peoria, Macomb, Quincy, Rochester, Springfield, Jacksonville, and Edwardsville.

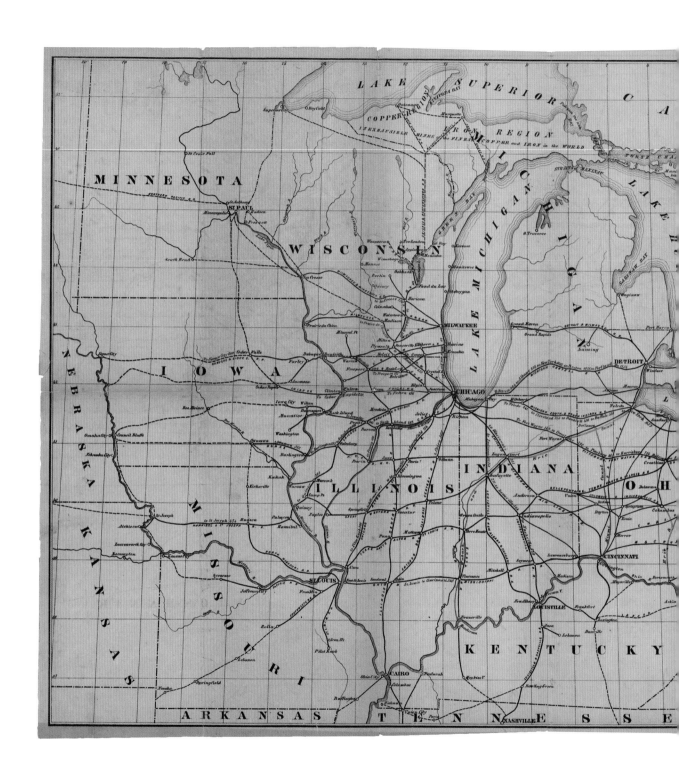

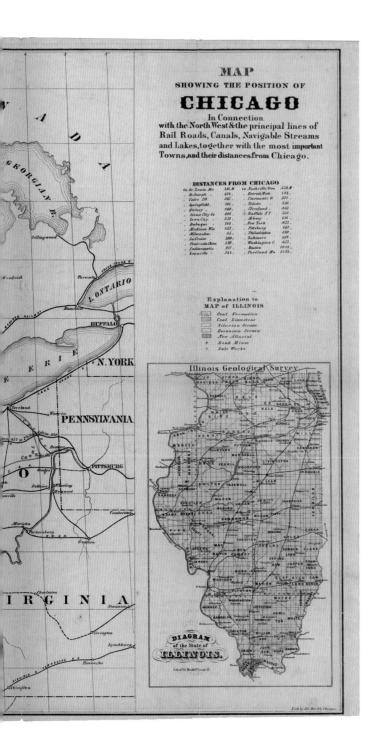

Edward Mendel, a lithographer living in Chicago, produced this map sometime during the 1850s. Railroads and canals were vital in the development of Chicago. Construction on the first railroad out of Chicago, the Galena and Chicago Union, began in 1848. That same year, the Illinois and Michigan Canal was completed, allowing boat transportation from the Great Lakes to the Mississippi River and the Gulf of Mexico. The expansion of railroads across the country eventually reduced the importance of the canal, which ceased transportation operations in 1933. The lower right corner of the map depicts an Illinois Geological Survey. Areas of coal formation are shown, along with lead mines and salt works.

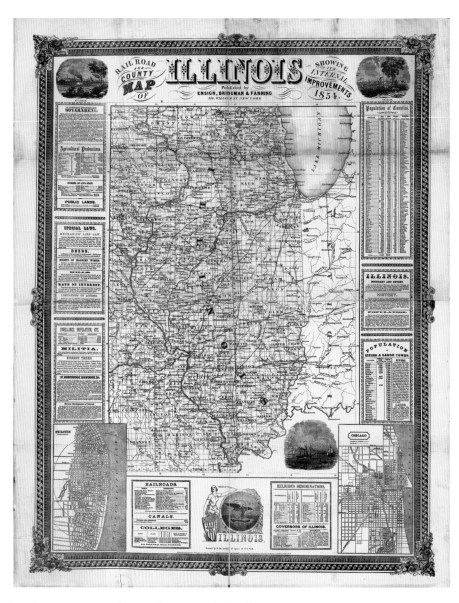

Rail road and county map of Illinois showing its internal improvements—
Ensign, Bridgman & Fanning (1854)

By 1853 railroads had begun to displace stagecoaches, steamboats, and freight wagons in Illinois. The rail system grew rapidly between 1850 and 1860. Railways were instrumental in the development of the state, allowing easy transportation of farm produce, mineral ore, and coal. This detailed map published by Ensign, Bridgman, and Fanning in 1854, depicts drainage, place names, roads, and railroads. Text on each side and at the bottom of the map provides information about the state's history, boundaries, population, colleges, government, agricultural production, and religious denominations. Insets also include street maps of Chicago and St. Louis.

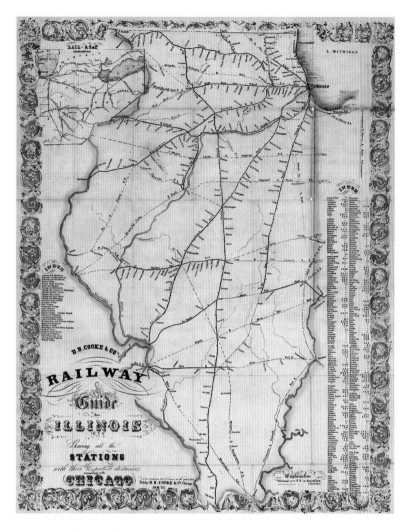

Railway guide for Illinois shewing [sic] all the stations with their respective distances connecting with Chicago—D. B. Cooke & Co. (1855)

Published by D. B. Cooke and Company of Chicago in 1855, this railway guide provides an index listing the names of railroad lines and an index listing towns and the railroads that serve them. For example, Decatur is served by "G W" (Great Western) and Peoria is served by "B V" (Bureau Valley). The Explanation near the lower right corner tells us that the bold, heavy lines show "R.R. in operation" and the lighter, dashed lines show "R.R. in progress." Historically, the first railroad out of Chicago was the Galena and Chicago Union, chartered in 1836 to build tracks to the lead mines at Galena. The Illinois Central Railroad (ICR) was chartered in 1851 to build a railroad from Cairo to Galena, with a branch from Centralia to Chicago (known as the "Chicago Branch"). Completed in 1856, the ICR gave Chicago a route to New Orleans by way of a railroad-operated steamboat line between Cairo and New Orleans.

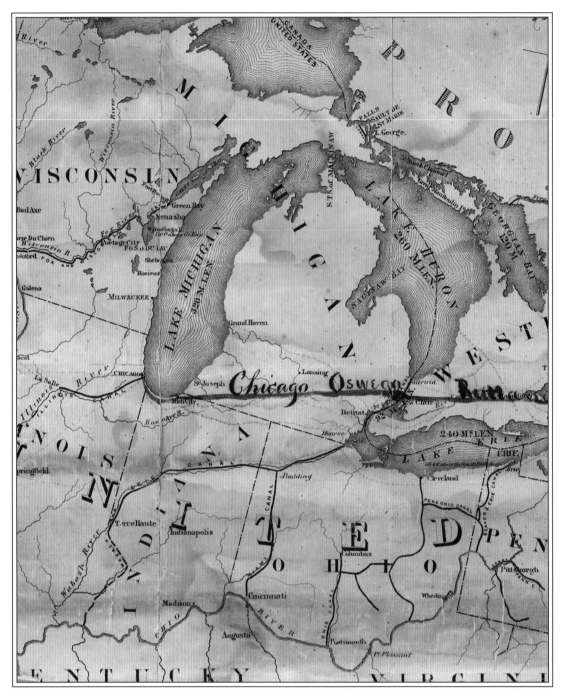

Detail from map on pages 48 and 49

"Now We Are Engaged in a Great Civil War"

THREE STATES CLAIM AMERICA'S SIXTEENTH president as their own: Kentucky, where he was born; Indiana, where he spent his youth; and Illinois, where he lived during the thirty years before he was elected president. So close is the connection between Abraham Lincoln and Illinois that the state's slogan is "Land of Lincoln."

Thirteen members of the Lincoln family, including twenty-one-year-old Abe, arrived in Macon County, Illinois, in 1830. The following year, Lincoln moved to New Salem (about thirty miles northwest of Springfield). Largely self-educated, he became known as a hard worker and gifted storyteller. In 1834 he was elected to the Illinois House of Representatives. His experiences there led him to pursue a law degree, which he received in 1836. He filed his first plea in his first suit in the Sangamon County Circuit Court on October 5, 1836.

Instrumental in efforts to transfer the state capital from Vandalia to Springfield, Lincoln moved to Springfield himself to practice law in 1837. His political star ascended rapidly. After being reelected to the Illinois legislature four times, he was elected in 1846 as a representative from Illinois to the Thirtieth Congress of the United States.

His next goal was a seat in the U.S. Senate, but he lost that contest to Stephen A. Douglas in 1858. Fortunately for Lincoln, a series of debates with Douglas raised his political profile not only in Illinois but nationwide.

At the 1860 National Convention of the Republican Party, held in Chicago, Abraham Lincoln received the party's nomination for president of the United States. Although Lincoln swept the populous northern states in the election that year, he was not even on the ballot in most southern states. Republicans were "as scarce as hen's teeth" in the South, and no one was willing to stick his neck out to put Lincoln's name on a southern ballot.

Throughout most of the 1850s the nation had been divided on questions of states' rights and slavery in the territories. Illinois was a "free" state, but those who had owned slaves before Illinois joined the Union were allowed to keep them. Slavery was allowed for owners of salt mines, who needed a source of cheap labor to remain in operation.

Following Lincoln's inauguration in March of 1861, a number of southern states seceded from the Union, and soon the country was "engaged in a great civil war," as Lincoln himself phrased it in his Gettysburg Address.

The Lincoln-Illinois connection is so strong in our minds today that we may be inclined to think the state was 100 percent pro-Lincoln and pro-Union during the Civil War. This assumption does not take into account the fact that 30 to 40 percent of the population of Illinois in 1860 consisted of people from the Upper South. Only two other "politically northern" states—Ohio and Indiana—had such a large concentration of southerners within their borders.

Southerners living in Illinois harbored an intense dislike for the "Puritans" who had settled in the northern part of the state. The families who had settled in southern Illinois had more ties to Dixie than New England in terms of ancestry, religious beliefs, and lifestyle. They also tended to support the idea that any state or states should be free to withdraw from the Union at any time. Lincoln was determined to preserve the Union.

In the weeks before South Carolina seceded from the Union, a newspaper in Cairo, Illinois, declared that it was not in favor of the "perpetuation of the Union by force," adding: "So far as our observations have extended, the sympathies of our people are mainly with the South." A Belleville publication asserted: "To submit then, or secede, is forced upon the South. Thus far, they have justice and right on their side."

On the Illinois state seal, the words "State Sovereignty—National Union" were placed so that "National Union" was most prominent. Illinois lived up to this motto. The state not only remained in the Union, but responded to every call for troops, even exceeding its quota. Although no battles were fought on Illinois soil, preparation for combat took place in training camps all across the state. At the request of Washington, D.C., Governor Richard Yates sent troops to

protect Cairo, a port city and railroad hub. The nearby town of Mound City was chosen by the U.S. Navy as its principal freshwater depot.

Prison camps brought captured soldiers into Illinois towns such as Alton, Springfield, Chicago, and Rock Island. The estate of Stephen A. Douglas, who died in 1861, provided land for Camp Douglas near Lake Michigan. Camp Douglas served as a major mustering-in site early in the war and later as a prisoner-of-war camp.

Of the 177 generals supplied to the Union Army by Illinois, the most prominent was West Point graduate Ulysses S. Grant. Born in Ohio, Grant fought under General Zachary Taylor in the Mexican War. In 1860 he moved to Galena, Illinois, to work in his father's leather store. Initially appointed to command a volunteer regiment, he rose through the ranks and in 1864 was appointed General in Chief of all U.S. armies. He later served two terms as president of the United States.

In addition to providing manpower, Illinois supported the Union cause by contributing farm products. As a major railroad hub, Chicago played a key role in the war effort as trains carried crops and livestock to market with all necessary speed. Chicago's position on Lake Michigan also served it well when the Union blockaded the South, and ships could no longer drop off goods to be sent to St. Louis.

The people of the Prairie State held sanitation fairs to raise money, much of which went to improve sanitation in military camps. Many Illinois women worked as nurses and aides in army camps. Galesburg widow Mary Ann "Mother" Bickerdyke responded to the needs of Northern soldiers by establishing more than three hundred field hospitals. Jennie Hodgers, a native of Ireland, left her home in Belvidere, Illinois, to enlist in the Union Army under the name Albert D. J. Cashier. She continued to pose as a man after the war and even voted in elections long before Illinois gave women the right to vote.

Pro-Confederate activities continued in parts of southern Illinois throughout the war. Lincoln once commented privately that he feared rebellion in Ohio, Indiana, and Illinois more than a purely military defeat. In March 1864 a riot erupted in Charleston, Illinois, when members of an Illinois infantry unit and a group of southern sympathizers began shooting at each other.

The level of divisiveness in the state and elsewhere did not bode well for Lincoln, who was running for reelection in 1864. Despite Lincoln's own misgivings about his chances, he defeated General George B. McClellan.

On April 9, 1865, Confederate commander Robert E. Lee surrendered to Ulysses S. Grant at Appomattox Court House, Virginia. Celebrations throughout the North were cut short a few days later, when Lincoln was assassinated by John Wilkes Booth at Ford's Theatre in Washington D.C.

Lincoln's funeral train stopped in Illinois at Chicago and at Springfield, its final destination. Funeral services were held in Springfield on May 4, 1865. Lincoln's tomb in Oak Ridge Cemetery is the final resting place of Abraham Lincoln, his wife Mary, and three of their four sons, Edward, William, and Thomas. (The eldest, Robert T., is buried in Arlington National Cemetery.)

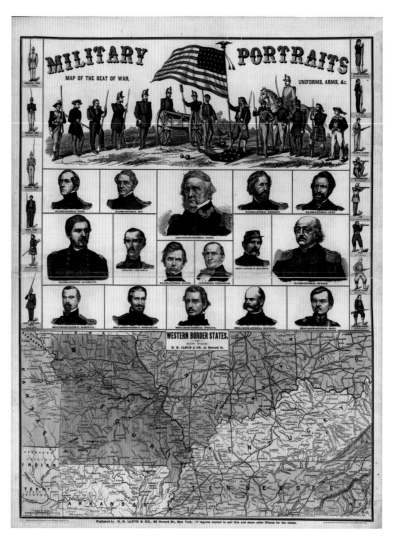

Western border states—Hall (ca. 1861)

Subtitled "Map of the Seat of War" and "Uniforms, Arms, etc.," the top half of this sheet shows military portraits, uniforms, and arms used by Union forces during the Civil War. The small figures on either side are labeled with the branch of the armed services as well as the military commands being demonstrated. Pictured in portrait form are Generals Wool, Dix, Scott, Fremont, Lyon, McClellan, Banks, Blenker, Butler, McDowell, Rosecrans (here spelled "Rosencranz"), Sprague, Burnside, and Sigel, Colonel Corcoran, and Commodore Stringham. The lower section—"Western Border States"—is a map of Missouri, Tennessee, and parts of Nebraska, Kansas, Indian Territory, Arkansas, Illinois, Indiana, Ohio, Kentucky, Virginia, North Carolina, and South Carolina, showing cities and towns, rivers, and railroads. Important or strategic places are underlined in red or indicated by red dots. The sheet, published in 1861, was illustrated by Edward S. Hall and published by H. H. Lloyd and Company.

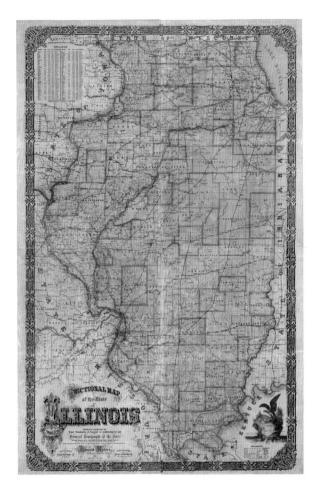

Sectional map of the state of Illinois, especially exhibiting the exact boundaries of counties as established by law and the general topography of the state as towns, streams, lakes, ponds, bluffs, rail-roads, state- & common-roads & tc. also the main coal field, mineral districts, outcrops of coalbanks, mines & tc.—— Compiled & drawn from the government—state—geological—topographical and many other most authentic documents of Leopold Richter, State Topographer, Springfield, Ill.; engraved on stone and printed by Leopold Gast, Brother & Co. St. Louis, Mo. (1861)

Compiled and drawn by state topographer Leopold Richter and published in 1861, this detailed map shows relief by hachures, drainage, minerals, township and county boundaries, cities and towns, roads, railroads, streams, lakes, ponds, and bluffs. The map also indicates the main coalfield, mineral districts, outcrops of coal banks, and mines. The depiction of the "Pike County Rail Road" (linking Naples, Illinois, with Hannibal, Missouri, and the Mississippi River) was likely conjectural and based on working plans for its path. Although the Pike County Rail Road Company was formed in 1853, the railroad wasn't built until 1869.

Bird's eye view of junction of the Ohio & Mississippi Rivers,
showing Cairo and part of the southern states—
Bachmann (1861)

Swiss-born lithographer and artist John Bachmann Sr. was best known for his bird's-eye views. This panoramic map published in 1861 looks south from Vienna, Illinois, to Holly Springs, Mississippi. Waverly, Tennessee, is on the left and Poplar Bluff, Missouri, is on the right. Distances from Cairo, Illinois, to various towns are listed in the bottom margin. During the Civil War, Cairo was the site for a huge Union military camp and supply depot. Troops and war materiel from across the Northwest came through Cairo to be sent down-river to support General Grant's troops as far south as Vicksburg. This map shows the military encampment and fortifications at Cairo, plus roads, railroads, rivers, towns, relief, and woodland.

Distance from

Cairo to Batesville 230 Miles
Memphis 265
Little Rock 325

Drawn from Nature and Lith. by John Bachmann

Entered according to act of Congress in the year 1861 by John Bachmann, in the Clerks Office of the District Court of the U.S. for the Southern District of New York.

BIRD'S EYE VIEW OF
JUNCTION OF THE OHIO & MISSISSIPPI RIVERS,
SHOWING CAIRO AND PART OF THE SOUTHERN STATES.

A. Rumpf, Publisher 175 Broadway.
Agent for John Bachmann's Publications.
NEW YORK.

Distance from:

Cairo to Poplar Bluff	75 Miles
Jackson	105
Paris	170

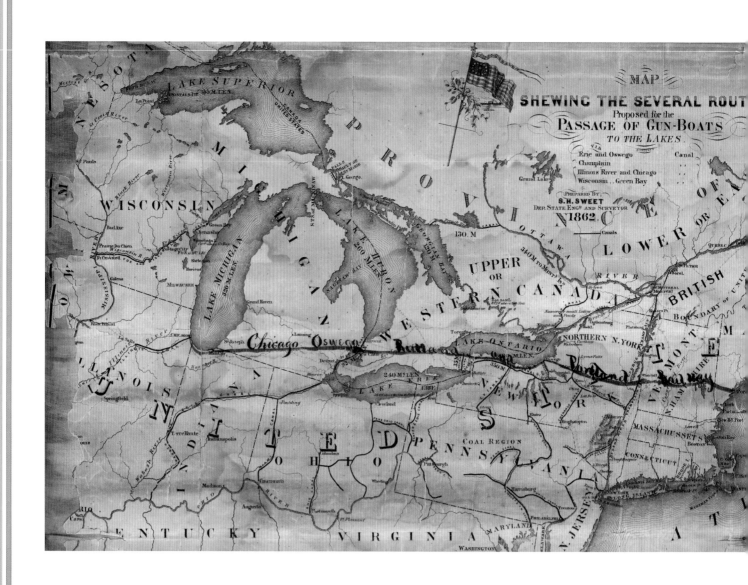

Map shewing [sic] the several routes proposed for the passage of gunboats to the Lakes via: Erie and Oswego Canal; Champlain [Canal]; Illinois River and Chicago [Canal]; Wisconsin, Green Bay [Canal]—Sweet (1862)

S. H. Sweet, deputy state engineer for New York, prepared this map showing canals and navigation routes in the northeastern United States and southeastern Canada. Published in 1862 by Charles Van Benthuysen of Albany, the map was designed specifically to indicate the location of several canals—the Erie and Oswego, Champlain, Illinois River and Chicago (Illinois and Michigan), and Wisconsin, Green Bay—all of which connected to the Great Lakes. The Illinois and Michigan Canal allowed boat transportation from the Great Lakes to the Mississippi River and the Gulf of Mexico. During the Civil War, the Union blockaded the South, and ships could no longer drop off goods to be sent to St. Louis. The Illinois and Michigan Canal, which opened in 1848, had already drawn some trade from St. Louis to Chicago. Due to the importance of the canal during the war, Chicago shot past St. Louis into the position of "capital of the Midwest."

1. *Military Prison,*
2. *Rebel Hospital,*
3. *Garrison Barracks,*
4. *Officers Quarters,*
5. *Post Hospital,*
6. *Garrison Barracks,*

Lith C. Vogt. H.Lambach del. Davenport.Io.

Entered according to Act of Congress in the year 1864 by C.Speidel in the Clerks Office of the District Court of the U.S. in and for the Northern District of Illinois.

Publ. by C.Speidel. Rock Island . Ill.

ROCK ISLAND BARRACKS, ILL

Rock Island Barracks, Ill.—Speidel (1864)

Rock Island is an island in the Mississippi River, as well as an Illinois city near the island. Rock Island Prison was situated on the island, which was owned by the U.S. government. The Rock Island barracks was first used as a prisoner-of-war camp in 1863. During the war it held a total of twelve thousand Confederate prisoners. This drawing of the prison includes a list of principal buildings and features, keyed by number to the appropriate position in the view, including the Rebel Hospital, Officers Quarters, and Guard Houses. The lithograph by C. Vogt and H. Lambach was published by C. Speidel in 1864.

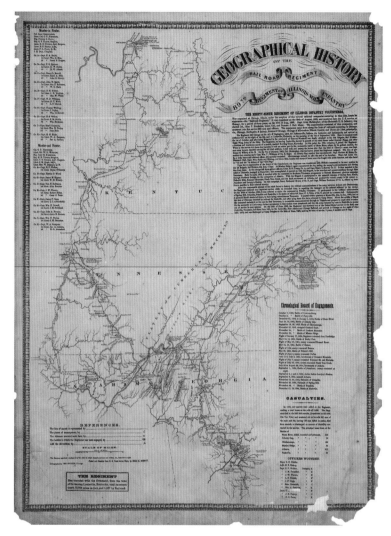

Geographical history of the rail road regiment, 89th regiment of Illinois vols. infantry—
Platted and compiled from U.S. Coast Survey maps by Isaac N. Merritt (1862–65)

This map depicts the operations of the Eighty-Ninth regiment of Illinois volunteers during the Civil War. Parts of Kentucky, Tennessee, Alabama, and Georgia are shown. The Eighty-ninth Illinois infantry was organized in Chicago under the auspices of several railroad companies, and was therefore given the nickname "The Railroad Regiment." Included on the map are a "muster-in" and "muster-out" roster of officers, a "chronological record of engagements," a table of casualties, the names of officers wounded, and a brief history of the regiment. The map was platted and compiled by Isaac N. Merritt, a member of company H of "The Railroad Regiment." The year of publication is not known.

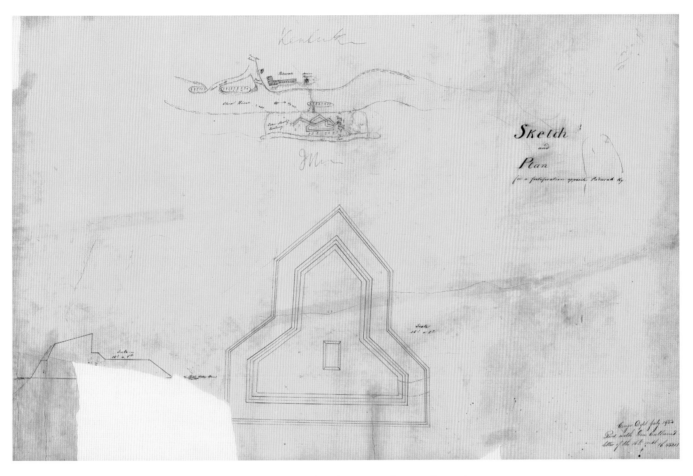

Sketch and plan for a fortification opposite Paducah, Ky.—unknown (1864)

In September 1861, forces under Union general Ulysses S. Grant captured Paducah, Kentucky, giving the Union control of the mouth of the Tennessee River, which flows into the Ohio River at Paducah. In March 1864 Confederate general Nathan Bedford Forrest raided Paducah. However, the Union remained in control of the town until the end of the war. Published in 1864, this sketch looks south across the Ohio River toward Paducah, showing the environs of a proposed fort in Massac County, Illinois. Relief is shown by hachures. A small map of Paducah, Kentucky, is included. The writing in the lower right corner reads: "Engr. Dept., July 18/64. Recd. with Gen. Cullum's letter of the 16th inst. (C5621)."

Detail from map on pages 58 and 59

The Gilded Age and the Great Depression

THE LAST DECADES OF THE NINETEENTH CENTURY were a time of rapid and relentless change for Illinois. Extraordinary transformations took place on nearly every front. Long before the end of the century, railroad tracks crisscrossed the state. The trains that traveled on them carried grain, coal, building materials, farm implements, pottery, and clothing from Illinois towns to points east, west, north, and south.

By 1850 the state's livestock industry had come into its own. A decade later, Illinois was shipping more beef cattle to New York City than all other states combined. In the 1860s Chicago became the nation's leading meat-processing center.

The 1870s saw the establishment of the first large-scale mail order business by Chicago merchant Aaron Montgomery Ward. The McCormick factory in Chicago cranked out reapers in record time. Chicago was not the only passenger on the train to advancement and improvement. By 1880 the industrial output from downstate Illinois equaled that of the entire state of Indiana.

Even as entrepreneurs ushered in what humorist Mark Twain referred to as the "Gilded Age," Illinois also struggled to overcome daunting challenges. The Great Chicago Fire of 1871 leveled Chicago's central business district, killing at least three hundred people and leaving another one hundred thousand homeless.

A financial panic in 1873 exacerbated an already tense labor situation in the state as workers were laid off or suffered pay cuts. Rail workers in East St. Louis went on strike in 1877, as did coal miners at Braidwood. A bombing in Chicago's Haymarket Square in 1886 drew national attention as anarchists and socialists demanded an end to capitalism.

Another severe economic depression in 1893 included abrupt declines in the stock market, bank closings, and business failures. Several major railroads went into receivership. The Pullman Strike of 1894, which began in Chicago with employees of the Pullman Palace Car Company, became a national railway strike. Also in 1894, coal miners in southeast Illinois refused to obey an agreement accepted by the United Mine Workers. The state militia was sent to various parts of the region on nine different occasions to control the violence.

Wealthy and middle-class Americans enjoyed the benefits of marvelous inventions during the 1890s. At the same time, countless men, women, and children lived in tenements and slums and worked endless hours in factories. In Chicago, as in many large cities, an enormous gulf existed between the privileged and the poor.

Jane Addams, a native of Cedarville, Illinois, responded to the deplorable conditions on Chicago's Near West Side by founding Hull House with her friend Ellen Gates Starr. Motivated by a visit to Toynbee Hall, a pioneering social settlement in London, Addams and Starr hoped to improve and enrich lives. Three years later, Illinois became the first state to establish an eight-hour work day and forty-eight-hour work week for children.

At the turn of the century the population of Illinois was 4,821,550—nearly one million more people than the state contained in 1890. The population of Decatur nearly tripled during the early decades of the twentieth century as the city became a national center for processing the raw materials of central Illinois for export. Soybeans moved into second place behind corn as a leading crop for the state.

More people meant more challenges, especially in Chicago, where waste management had become a major problem. In an engineering feat worthy of the front-page headlines it received, the flow of the Chicago River was reversed so that waste-laden water would flow south rather than into Lake Michigan.

Engineering social change was even more problematic. In 1905 socialist Eugene V. Debs and others founded the Industrial Workers of the World union in Chicago to "emancipate the working class." The plight of Chicago's working class took center stage in author Upton Sinclair's book *The Jungle* and William T. Stead's *If Christ Came to Chicago*.

Chicago was also home to a phenomenon known as "machine" or "boss" politics. Aldermen or "ward bosses" acquired power and money by selling their votes to the highest bidder. Unwilling to see corruption continue in local government, the Municipal Voters' League and other reformist groups helped elect progressive mayor Carter Harrison II in 1897.

In 1913 Illinois became the first state east of the Mississippi to grant women the right to vote in municipal and presidential elections. The "Illinois Law" became a model for suffrage laws in other states.

When the United States entered World War I in June 1917 by declaring war on Germany, Illinois was in a unique position. It contained more immigrants from Germany and Austria than any other state. In response to the declaration of war, German flags were hoisted aloft on Chicago's North Side and bands played German songs. Before long, however, anti-German propaganda and hostility motivated German Americans to pull their flags inside and, in some cases, to change their surnames.

Volunteers raised money and coordinated relief work. Illinois factories increased production to meet overseas demands for supplies. The resulting labor shortage prompted companies to seek additional employees. Local businessmen in East St. Louis recruited an estimated ten thousand African Americans from the South. In Chicago the African-American population doubled between 1910 and 1920. When World War I ended, racial violence in Illinois escalated. In many cases, hostility was related to the sudden influx of African Americans and competition for jobs.

Anyone who had envisioned the Land of Lincoln as a model of racial harmony was in for a rude awakening. In 1908 race riots and lynchings in Springfield resulted in the deaths of two blacks and four whites. Hundreds of thousands of dollars worth of property was destroyed. More than forty black families were displaced when their homes were burned, and dozens of citizens of both races were injured. The NAACP (National Association for the Advancement of Colored People) was formed partly in response to the 1908 race riots.

From 1919 to 1933 Illinois and the rest of the nation had their hands full with the effects of the Eighteenth Amendment, which prohibited the manufacture, sale, and transportation of intoxicating beverages. Bootlegging was common throughout the state. Southern Illinois had the Shelton Brothers Gang. Chicago had "Scarface" Al Capone, "Big Jim" Colosimo, Johnny "The Fox" Torio, "Bugs" Moran, and a host of other colorfully named, morally bankrupt gangsters.

Although we tend to focus on the violence and corruption that was rampant in Chicago during the Roaring Twenties, the city also emerged as a leading producer of commercial vehicles during that decade. In sports, the Decatur Staleys moved to Chicago and won a national football championship. They would later become the Chicago Bears. Aviator Charles Lindbergh began daily mail delivery between Chicago and St. Louis in 1926.

The repeal of Prohibition in 1933 was celebrated by many but not too extravagantly, given that the stock market had crashed four years earlier, plunging the nation into a severe depression. Even in Illinois—with its corn, wheat, and livestock—people went hungry. The Great Depression lasted into the early 1940s, causing catastrophic levels of unemployment across the state.

Yet all was not lost. In 1933 Chicago hosted A Century of Progress, an international exhibition celebrating the one hundredth anniversary of the city's incorporation. The fair focused on social, scientific, and technological progress. In 1937 oil was discovered in Marion County, starting an oil boom in southern Illinois. By the end of the year, Illinois ranked eleventh among oil producing states. It seemed that prosperity must be just around the corner.

Springfield, Illinois—Ruger (1867)

Drawn by pioneering panoramic-map artist Albert Ruger, this bird's-eye view of Springfield, Illinois, is oriented with north toward the upper right. Springfield's most famous past resident is Abraham Lincoln, who lived there from 1837 until he moved into the White House as President in 1861. Lincoln was instrumental in getting Springfield named as the state capital in 1839. The map is indexed for points of interest, including the state arsenal, ward schools, the state capitol building, the water works, churches, Lincoln's residence, and Lincoln's tomb, where Lincoln, his wife Mary Todd Lincoln, and three of their four sons are buried. Like most panoramic maps, this one is not drawn to scale. The artist's focus was on street patterns, individual buildings, and landscape features.

SPRINGFIELD
ILLINOIS 1867.

CHICAGO LITHOGRAPHING CO.

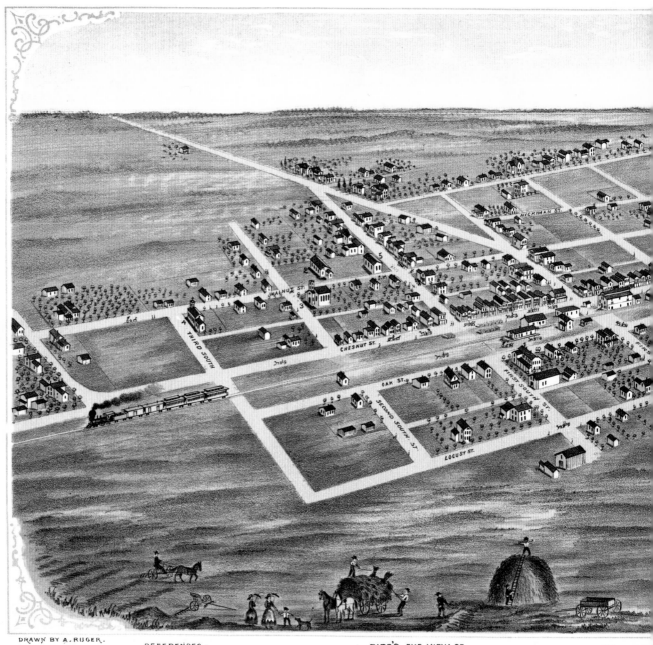

DRAWN BY A. RUGER.

REFERENCES:

Nº 1. DEPOT.
" 2. SCHOOL HOUSE.

BIRD'S EYE VIEW OF

MANTENO.

KANKAKEE COUNTY ILLINOIS
1869.

Nº 3 PRESB
" 4 CATHO
" 5. METHO

MERCHANTS' LITHOGR.C° CHICAGO.
AN CHURCH

Bird's eye view of Manteno, Kankakee County, Illinois—Ruger (1869)

Albert Ruger's panoramic map of Manteno, Illinois, was published in 1869 by Merchant's Lithographing Company of Chicago. That same year, Manteno, located approximately forty miles south of Chicago's Loop, was incorporated as a village. The name Manteno was derived from that of Mawteno (or Mon-te-no), daughter of Francois Bourbonnais Jr. and Catish, his Indian wife. Bourbonnais was the son of Francois Bourbonnais Sr., a fur trapper, hunter, and agent of the American Fur Company. Points of interest indexed at the bottom of the drawing include a train depot, schoolhouse, and churches. Like most panoramic maps, this one is not drawn to scale.

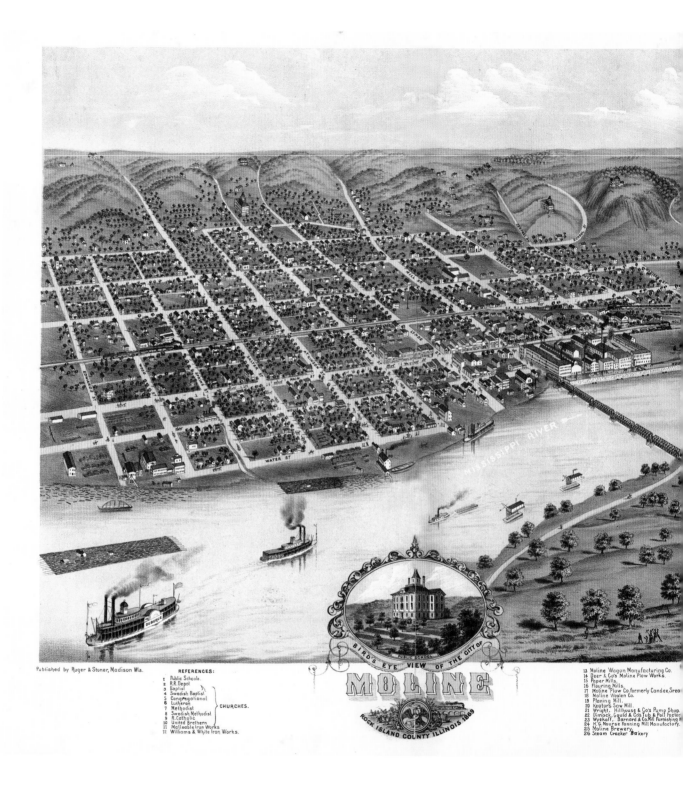

Published by Ruger & Stoner, Madison Wis.

REFERENCES:

1   Public Schools.
2   R.R. Depot
3   Baptist
4   Swedish Baptist
5   Congregational
6   Lutheran
7   Methodist   } CHURCHES.
8   Swedish Methodist
9   R. Catholic
10 United Brethern
11 Malleable Iron Works
12 Williams & White Iron Works.

13 Moline Wagon Manufacturing Co.
14 Deer & Co's Moline Plow Works.
15 Paper Mills.
16 Flouring Mills.
17 Moline Plow Co. formerly Candee, Srea
18 Moline Woolen Co.
19 Planing Mill.
20 Keator's Saw Mill.
21 Wright, Hillhouse & Co's Pump Shop.
22 Dimock, Gould & Co's Tub & Pail Factor
23 Wyckoff, Barnard & Co. Mill Furnishing
24 H. G. Nourse Fanning Mill Manufactory.
25 Moline Brewery.
26 Steam Cracker Bakery.

BIRD'S EYE VIEW OF THE CITY OF
PUBLIC SCHOOL.

MOLINE

ROCK ISLAND COUNTY ILLINOIS 1869

Lithogr. Co. S. Clark St. N° 152 & 154.

Bird's eye view of the city of Moline, Rock Island County, Illinois—Ruger (1869)
Moline is one of the Quad Cities, along with neighboring Rock Island in Illinois and the cities of Davenport and Bettendorf in Iowa. It is located between the banks of the Mississippi River and Rock River. After the Civil War, the city's street grid was expanded to the east and west along the shoreline and to the south up the bluffs. This bird's-eye view was created by panoramic artist Albert Ruger and his partner, Joseph J. Stoner. The map is indexed for points of interest, including public schools, the railroad depot, churches, paper mills, and factories. The map was published in 1869 by Chicago Lithographing Company. Like most panoramic maps, this one is not drawn to scale.

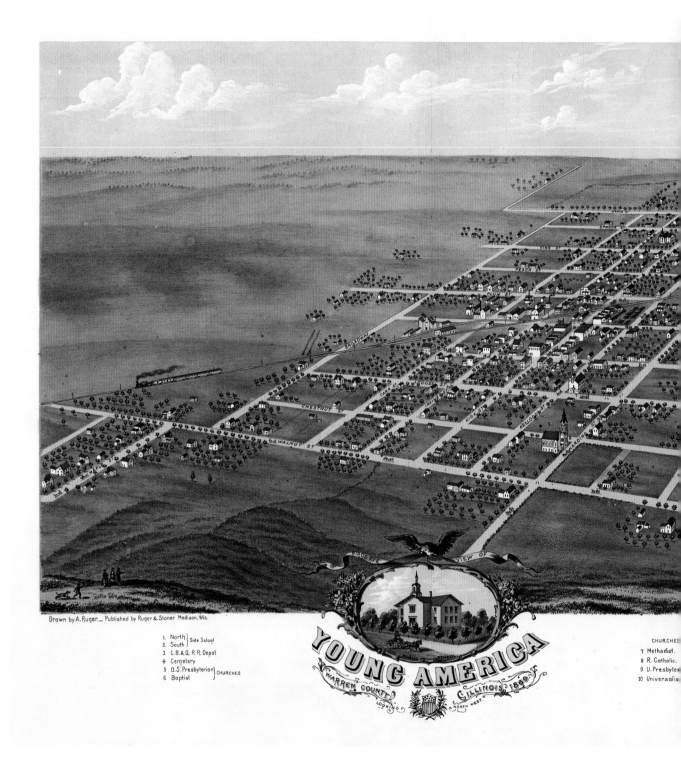

Drawn by A. Ruger._ Published by Ruger & Stoner Madison, Wis.

1. North } Side School
2. South
3 C.B.& Q. R.R. Depot
4 Cemetery
5 O.S. Presbyterian } CHURCHES
6 Baptist

CHURCHES
7 Methodist.
8 R. Catholic.
9 U. Presbyter
10 Universalis

YOUNG AMERICA

WARREN COUNTY   ILLINOIS 1869

LOOKING   NORTH WEST.

Chicago Lith. Co. S. Clark St. Chicago.

Bird's eye view of Young America, Warren County, Illinois—Ruger (1869)
First platted in 1854, Young America was incorporated in 1865. This bird's-eye view, published in 1869 by Chicago Lithographing Company, was created by panoramic artist Albert Ruger, whose partner was Joseph J. Stoner. The view faces west. Points of interest indexed at the bottom of the drawing include the North and South Side schools, the railroad depot, the cemetery, and churches. In 1874 the town name was changed to Kirkwood in honor of the Civil War governor of Iowa, Samuel J. Kirkwood, who was greatly admired by the residents of Young America. Like most panoramic maps, this one is not drawn to scale.

*Bird's eye view of the city of Urbana, Champaign County, Illinois—
Ruger (1869)*

Albert Ruger's panoramic map of Urbana, Illinois, was published in 1869 by Chicago Lithographing Company. The map is indexed for points of interest, including the courthouse, county jail, railroad depot, cemetery, churches, and Industrial University. Industrial University, which opened for classes in 1868, eventually became the University of Illinois at Urbana-Champaign. Two years after this map was published, in 1871, much of downtown Urbana burned to the ground. Like the Great Chicago Fire that same year, the Great Urbana Fire started in a stable. Like most panoramic maps, this one is not drawn to scale.

BIRD'S EYE VIEW OF THE CITY OF

URBANA
CHAMPAIGN COUNTY ILLINOIS
1869

1 Court House
2 County Jail
3 Industrial University
4 Public School
5 I.B.&W.R.W. Depot
6 Cemetery

CHURCHES.
7 Baptist
8 Methodist
9 Presbyterian
10 R. Catholic

COURT HOUSE.

Chicago Lithogr's Co. S. Clark St. Chicago.

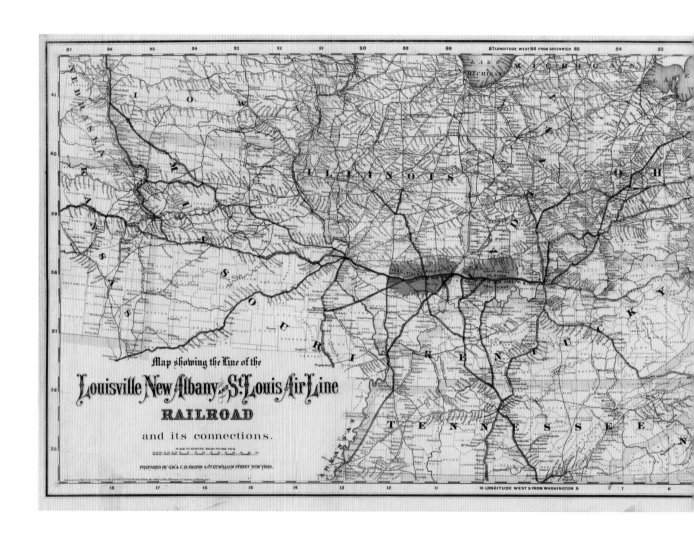

Map showing the Line of the

Louisville New Albany and St Louis Air Line
RAILROAD
and its connections.

SCALE 35 STATUTE MILES TO ONE INCH.

PREPARED BY G.W. & C.B. COLTON & CO 172 WILLIAM STREET NEW YORK.

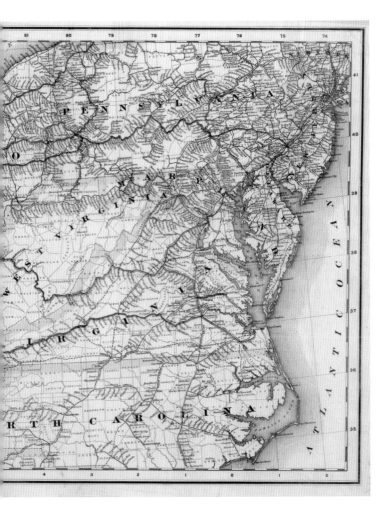

Map showing the line of the Louisville, New Albany, and St. Louis Air Line Railroad and its connections—Colton & Co. (1872)

Published in 1872 by G. W. and C. B. Colton and Company, this map of the middle Atlantic and central United States shows drainage, cities and towns, state and county boundaries, and the railroad network with emphasis on the main lines. The map also indicates coalfields in Illinois and Indiana. As early as 1673, French explorers Louis Jolliet and Father Jacques Marquette reported seeing coal along the banks of the Illinois River near Ottawa (LaSalle County). In 1810 a small mine near Murphysboro (Jackson County) produced the first commercial sale of coal from an Illinois coal mine. The town of Braidwood (Will County) was founded when a rich vein of coal was discovered in 1865. The names of a number of Illinois towns—for example, Coal City, Carbon Hill, and Diamond (named after "black diamonds," or coal)—reflect the importance of coal mining in the state.

*The City of Chicago as it was before the great conflagration
of October 8th, 9th, & 10th, 1871—Flint (ca. 1872)*

Incorporated as a city in 1837, Chicago experienced phenomenal growth with the arrival of the railroads. By 1871 the population was approximately 334,000. This bird's-eye view, published in 1872 by William Flint, looks southwest from Lake Michigan. It includes the train depot and the Chicago River, which divides into its north and south branches near the top of the map. The Great Chicago Fire of 1871 destroyed well over seventeen thousand buildings, but Chicagoans soon started to rebuild the city. Just six weeks after the fire, construction of more than three hundred buildings had already begun. Like most panoramic maps, this one is not drawn to scale.

AS IT WAS BEF

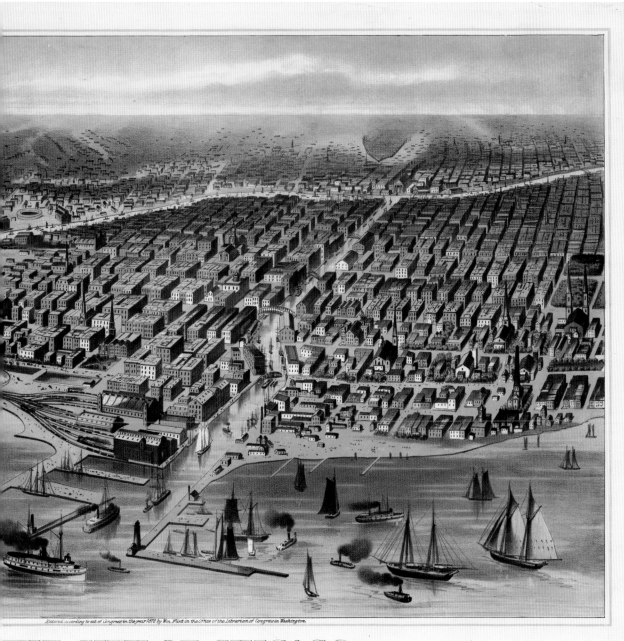

Entered according to act of Congress in the year 1872 by Wm. Flint in the Office of the Librarian of Congress in Washington.

THE CITY OF CHICAGO

THE GREAT CONFLAGRATION OF OCTOBER 8TH, 9TH & 10TH 1871.

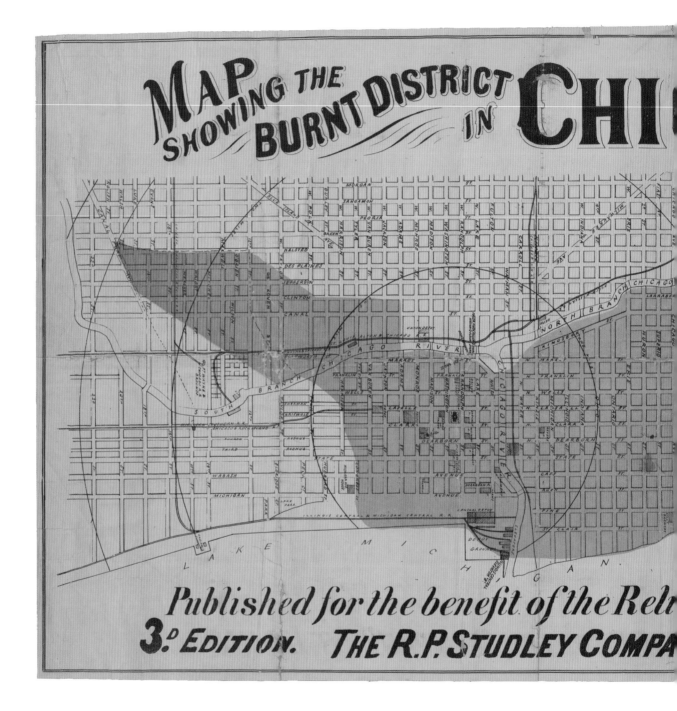

MAP SHOWING THE BURNT DISTRICT IN CHIC...

Published for the benefit of the Reli...
3.ᴰ EDITION. THE R.P. STUDLEY COMPA...

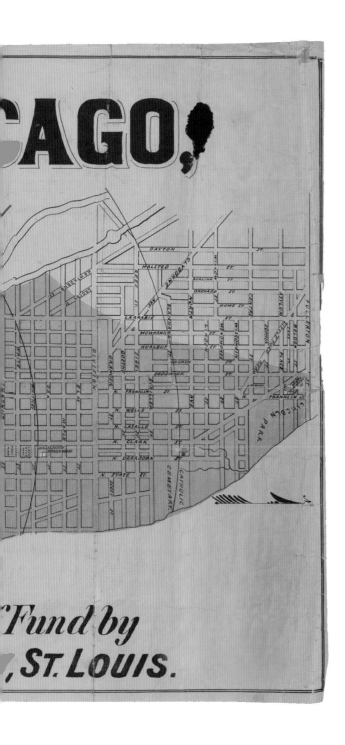

Map Showing the Burnt District in Chicago.
Published for the benefit of the Relief Fund by 3rd
Edition—The R.P. Studley Company, St. Louis (18--)
This map of Chicago first appeared in Colton's General Atlas of 1870 on the same page with a map of St. Louis. It was later overprinted with red coloring to show the area of Chicago burned in the Great Fire of 1871. The fire destroyed an area four miles long and three-quarters of a mile wide. During its thirty-six hours, it killed around three hundred people. Mrs. O'Leary's cow has long been relieved of the responsibility for this fire, but the actual origin is still unknown. The silver lining was that it prompted successful urban renewal efforts, led by a stronger fire code and fire-fighting force.

The City of Chicago—Parsons & Atwater (ca. 1874)

Within two years of the Great Fire of 1871, Chicago had been completely rebuilt. Charles Parsons and Lyman Atwater produced this bird's-eye view looking west over the city in 1874. Like most panoramic maps, this one is not drawn to scale. Published by Currier and Ives (Nathaniel Currier and James Ives), the map reveals that the new city was far superior to the old. Prominent features listed below the image include Dexter Race Course, Great Union Stock Yards, the entrance to the Chicago River, Great Central Depot, the Tremont House hotel, Humboldt Park, Lincoln Park, and a number of churches. By the time this map was published, Chicago's population had reached approximately 395,408—an increase of more than 61,000 over its population at the time of the Great Fire.

THE CITY OF CHICAGO.

NEW YORK. PUBLISHED BY CURRIER & IVES, 125 NASSAU ST.

New rail road map of the United States and the Dominion of Canada, showing the Chicago, Rock Island and Pacific R.R.; the great overland route and short line to the west and south-west— Heubach (1879)

This map of the United States by designer and engraver Emil Heubach shows relief by hachures, drainage, cities and towns, state boundaries, and the railroad network. The line was created by an act of the state of Illinois in 1847 and amended in 1851. The line reached the Mississippi River on February 22, 1854, where the first bridge to cross the river was opened on September 1, 1854, linking Rock Island with Davenport, Iowa. The Chicago, Rock Island and Pacific Railroad—better known as simply the Rock Island line—began as the Rock Island and La Salle Railroad Company, commissioned to connect Rock Island with the Illinois and Michigan Canal at La Salle.

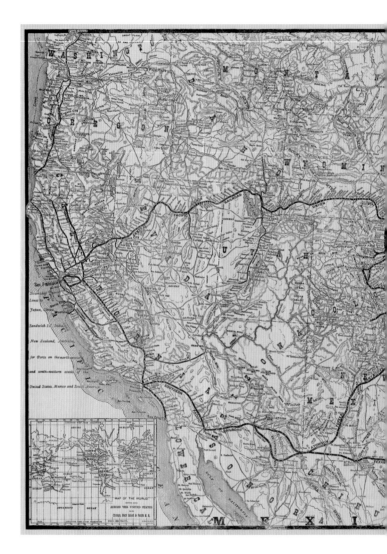

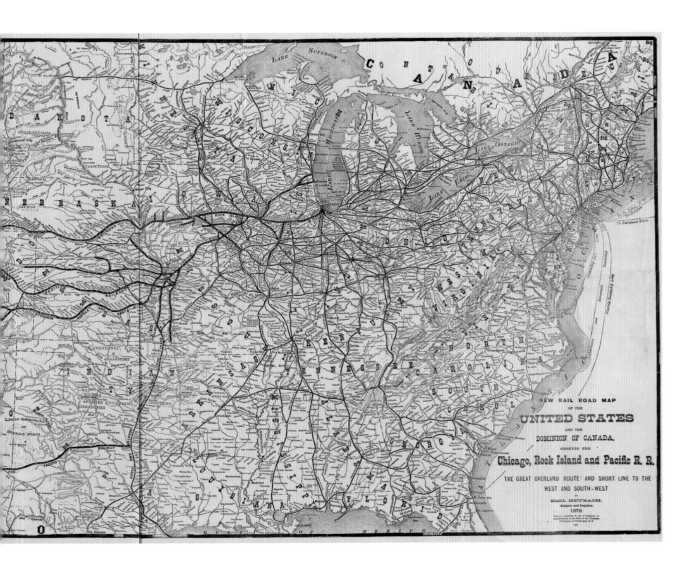

NEW RAIL ROAD MAP
OF THE
UNITED STATES
AND THE
DOMINION OF CANADA,
SHOWING THE
Chicago, Rock Island and Pacific R. R.
THE GREAT OVERLAND ROUTE AND SHORT LINE TO THE
WEST AND SOUTH-WEST
BY
EMIL HEUBACH,
Designer and Engraver.
1870.

Copyrighted by A.B. UPHAM, 1880.

ELGIN,
KANE CO., ILLINOIS.
1880.

Elgin, Kane Co., Illinois—Upham (1880)

Elgin is located about forty miles northwest of Chicago. This bird's-eye view of the town, drawn by A. B. Upham, was published in 1880 by Shober and Carqueville of Chicago. Like most panoramic maps, this one is not drawn to scale. The map identifies street names and points of interest, including the Elgin National Watch Works (shown in an inset in the upper left corner), the Northern Illinois State Mental Hospital (shown in an inset in the upper right corner), and the Fox River, a tributary of the Illinois River. In addition to the watch works, other industries contributed to Elgin's prosperity in the 1800s. Gail Borden's Elgin Milk Condensing Company started production in 1865. The Elgin Packing Company was incorporated in 1869. Joseph Vollar and Company began the manufacture of chewing gum in 1875. In 1882 the David C. Cook Publishing Company moved to Elgin, becoming the city's second-largest industrial employer by the end of 1883.

RASCHER'S BIRDS EYE VIEW OF THE CHICAGO PACKING HO
CHICAGO ILL.
SCALE OF BASELINE 100 FT. TO ONE INCH

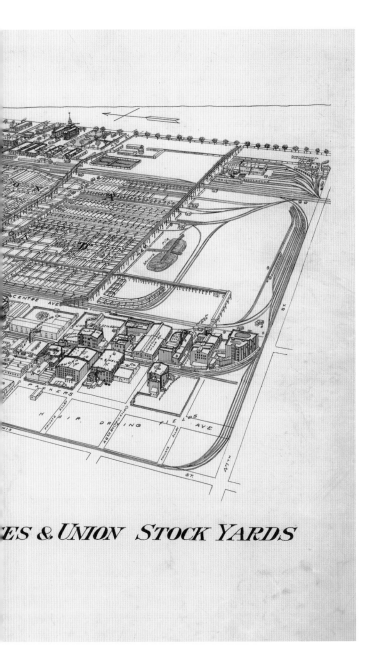

ES & UNION STOCK YARDS

Birds eye view of the Chicago packing houses &
union stock yards—Rascher (1890)

By 1864 Chicago had become a major railroad hub. A consortium of nine railroad companies purchased 320 acres of swampy land in southwest Chicago in order to build a centralized stockyard. Designed by civil engineer Octave Chanute, Union Stock Yard and Transit Company officially opened in 1865, and Union Stock Yards quickly became a significant commercial link between America's East and West. One of the earliest meat-packing companies to move into the area was the Armour plant in 1867. This panoramic view of Chicago's packing houses and Union Stock Yards, created in 1890 by Charles Rascher, a German surveyor who immigrated to Chicago sometime after 1871, looks northeast. The names of companies such as Armour, Swift and Company, and Fairbank Canning Company are inscribed on the roofs of the buildings. Like most panoramic maps, this one is not drawn to scale.

Bird's eye view of the World's Columbian Exposition, Chicago—Rand McNally and Company (1893)

The World's Columbian Exposition of 1893 occupied 630 acres in Jackson Park and the Midway Plaisance. The main site was bounded by Stony Island Avenue on the west, 67th Street on the south, Lake Michigan on the east, and 56th Street on the north. Landscape architect Frederick Law Olmsted was responsible for laying out the fairgrounds. More than two hundred buildings occupied the grounds. The fair introduced the world's first Ferris wheel as well as such products as Cracker Jacks, Juicy Fruit gum, and Cream of Wheat. Rand McNally and Company's bird's-eye view of the fair looks west and includes a list of attractions located by their coordinates on the map. Like most panoramic maps, this one is not drawn to scale.

BIRD'S-EY

COPYRIGHT, 1892, BY RAND, McNALLY & CO. PRINTERS, PUBLISHERS, AND ENGRAVERS. CHICAGO, JULY 28, 1892.

IEW OF THE WORLD'S COLUMBIAN EXPOSITION, CHICAGO, 1893.

R BUILDING. G-29.
DNIA. C-29.
GHT. I-23.
BUILDING. G-29.
NG. K-25.
NG. I-20.
STATION, INTRAMURAL RY. D-22.
HUNTERS' CAMP. H-15.
DOORS. E-23.
INTRAMURAL RY. V-4.

FRENCH BAKERY EXHIBIT. S-6.
FRENCH BUILDING. J-36.
FRENCH COLONIES EXHIBIT. V-4.
GERMAN BUILDING. K-35.
GREAT BRITAIN. M-35.
GREEN HOUSE. B-16.
GUATEMALIAN BUILDING. L-33.
HAITIEN BUILDING. M-34.
HOMEOPATHIC HEADQUARTERS. D-22.
HORTICULTURAL BUILDING. E-18.
ILLINOIS COOLING PLANT. E-6.
IDAHO STATE BUILDING. F-38.
ILLINOIS CENTRAL R. R. TRACKS. C-22.
ILLINOIS STATE BUILDING. E-27.

INDIANA STATE BUILDING. F-27.
INDIAN SCHOOL. I-14.
IOWA STATE BUILDING. G-40.
JAPANESE BUILDING. H-29.
JAPANESE TEA HOUSE. I-29.
KANSAS STATE BUILDING. I-23.
KENTUCKY STATE BUILDING. J-33.
KRUPP GUN EXHIBIT. V-5.
LIFE SAVING STATION. M-34.
LIGHT HOUSE EXHIBIT. M-31.
LOGGERS' CAMP. K-11.
LOUISIANA STATE BUILDING. H-35.
MACHINERY HALL. I-4.
MAINE STATE BUILDING. H-35.
MANUFACTURES AND LIBERAL ARTS BUILDING. M-15.

MARYLAND STATE BUILDING. G-37.
MASSACHUSETTS STATE BUILDING. G-37.
MERCHANT TAILORS' EXHIBIT. H-26.
MERCK & CO. DRUGS. D-22.
MICHIGAN STATE BUILDING. E-25.
MIDWAY PLAISANCE. B-16.
MIDWAY STATION, INTRAMURAL RY. D-23.
HINDS AND MINING BUILDING. G-22.
NORTH DAKOTA STATE BUILDING. D-29.
MINNESOTA STATE BUILDING. E-29.
MISSOURI STATE BUILDING. E-29.
MONTANA STATE BUILDING. F-38.
MOUNT VERNON STATION, INTRAMURAL RY. G-22.
MOVABLE SIDEWALK. X-24.
MUSIC HALL. S-18.
NAVAL EXHIBIT (BATTLE SHIP). O-23.

NAVAL OBSERVATORY. N-34.
NEBRASKA STATE BUILDING. D-34.
NEW HAMPSHIRE STATE BUILDING. H-39.
PHOTOGRAPH BUILDING. I-14.
NEW JERSEY STATE BUILDING. G-38.
NEW MEXICO, OKLA. AND ARIZ. JOINT TERRIT'L. BLDG. F-39.
NEW SOUTH WALES BUILDING. I-30.
NEW YORK STATE BUILDING. G-40.
NORTH DAKOTA STATE BUILDING. D-39.
NORTH LOOP, INTRAMURAL RY. L-23.
NORWEGIAN BUILDING. J-35.
OFFICE ELECTRICAL DEPARTMENT. K-1.
OHIO STATE BUILDING. E-26.
OIL HOUSE. D-1.
OKLAHOMA, ARIZ. AND NEW MEX. JOINT TERRIT'L BLDG. F-39.
PAINT SHOP. D-2.

PENNSYLVANIA STATE BUILDING. F-35.
PENNSYLVANIA R. R. EXHIBIT. K-5.
POLISH CAFÉ. X-19.
PUBLIC COMFORT BUILDING. H-24, I-29.
PUCK BUILDING. R-20.
PUMP HOUSE. E-5.
RHODE ISLAND STATE BUILDING. G-38.
SAW MILL. J-11.
SCALES OFFICE. D-2.
SERVICE BUILDING. D-15.
SHOE AND LEATHER EXHIBIT. W-4.
SIXTY-SECOND ST. STATION, INTRAMURAL RY. D-23.
SOUTH DAKOTA STATE BUILDING. D-29.
SOUTH LOOP, INTRAMURAL RY. U-5.

S. & R. T. STATION. E-7.
SPANISH BUILDING. J-35.
STOCK PAVILION. E-4.
SWEDISH BUILDING. J-36.
SWEDISH RESTAURANT. J-30.
TERMINAL STATION. G-5.
TEXAS STATE BUILDING. D-29.
TRANSPORTATION BUILDING. F-16.
TURKISH BUILDING. I-31.
UNITED STATES GOVERNMENT BUILDING. E-26.
U. S. WIND ENGINE AND PUMP CO. E-4.
UTAH TERRITORIAL BUILDING. D-27.
VANDERBILT R. R. EXHIBIT. D-2.
VAN HOUTEN & ROON PAVILION. G-26.

VENEZUELAN BUILDING. J-36.
VERMONT STATE BUILDING. H-38.
VIRGINIA STATE BUILDING. G-39.
WALTER M. LOWNEY CO.'S PAVILION. S-16.
WASHINGTON STATE BUILDING. D-39.
WEATHER BUREAU. M-35.
WELLINGTON CATERING CO. S-14.
WEST VIRGINIA STATE BUILDING. F-36.
WHALING BOAT FISHERIES (MUSEUM). V-3.
WHITE HORSE INN. Q-6.
WHITE STAR LINE BUILDING. N-32.
WISCONSIN STATE BUILDING. D-39.
WOMAN'S BUILDING. B-22.
W. C. E BARN. D-4.

ALL ELEVATED TRAINS IN CHICAGO
STOP AT THE
Chicago Rock Island and Pacific Railway Station
ONLY ONE ON THE LOOP

ELEVATED STATION | AT THE "ROCK ISLAND" | VAN BUREN ST. STATION.

W. H. TRUESDALE,
Vice-President and General Manager.

JOHN SEBASTIAN,
General Passenger and Ticket Agent.

All elevated trains in Chicago stop at the Chicago Rock Island and Pacific Railway Station, only one on the Loop—Poole Bros. (ca. 1897)

Published in 1897 by Poole Brothers, this bird's-eye view looks southwest over a portion of Chicago, showing the elevated railway system and Loop in connection with the Chicago, Rock Island and Pacific, and Lake Shore and Michigan Southern railway stations. Rock Island ticket offices and stations are listed. The map also includes an inset illustration of the "Elevated station at the 'Rock Island' Van Buren St. station" and indexes to points of interest such as hotels, dry goods and department stores, office buildings, public buildings, and theaters. A label at the bottom of the map bears the names of W. H. Truesdale (Vice President and General Manager) and John Sebastian (General Passenger and Ticket Agent) of the Chicago, Rock Island and Pacific Railroad. Like most panoramic maps, this one is not drawn to scale.

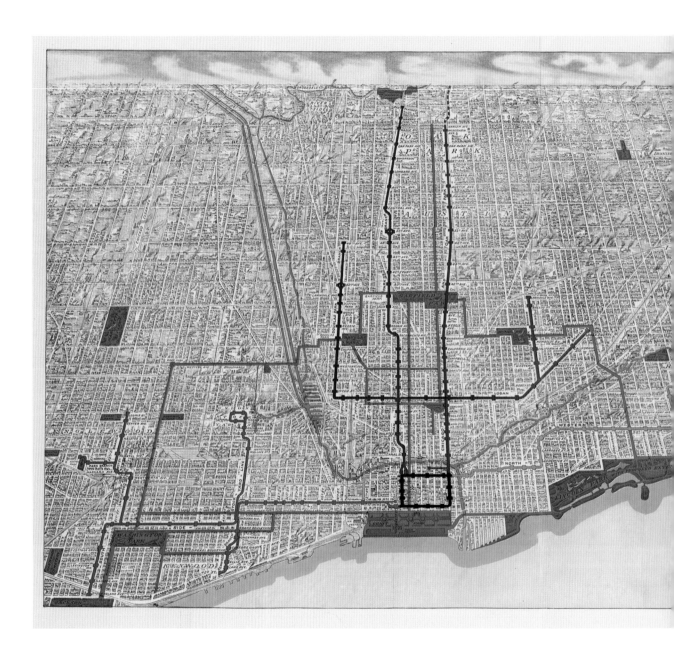

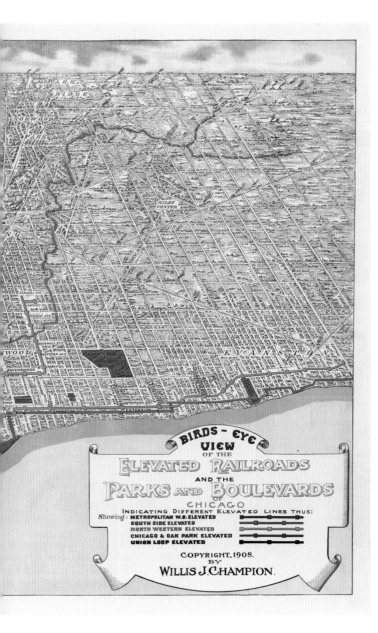

*Birds-Eye View of the Elevated Railroads and
the Parks and Boulevards of Chicago—
Champion (1908)*

This map published in 1908 by Willis J. Champion provides a birds-eye view of Chicago's elevated railroads, parks, and boulevards. Individual color-coded elevated lines include the Metropolitan W.S. (West Side) Elevated (the first "L" to be opened using electric traction technology), the South Side Elevated (Chicago's first rapid transit line), the North Western Elevated , the Chicago & Oak Park Elevated, and the Union Loop Elevated. Streets, parks, and neighborhoods such as Englewood, Kenwood, Ravenswood, and Oak Park are also labeled on the map. The first elevated line opened in 1892. By 1909 Chicago had one of the best rapid transit systems in the world.

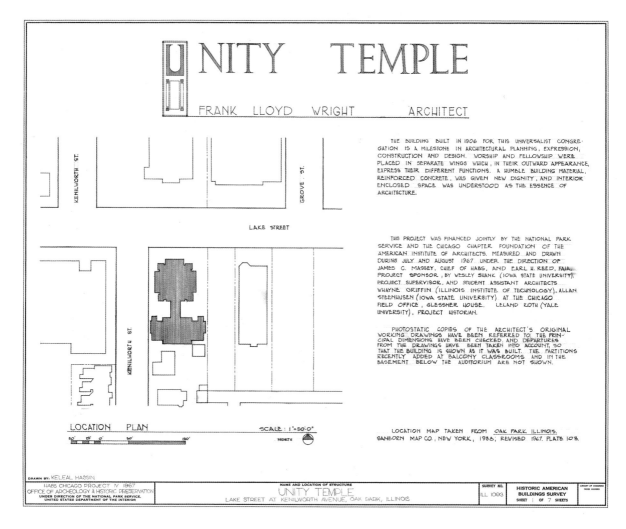

UNITY TEMPLE
FRANK LLOYD WRIGHT   ARCHITECT

THE BUILDING BUILT IN 1906 FOR THIS UNIVERSALIST CONGRE-
GATION IS A MILESTONE IN ARCHITECTURAL PLANNING, EXPRESSION,
CONSTRUCTION AND DESIGN. WORSHIP AND FELLOWSHIP WERE
PLACED IN SEPARATE WINGS WHICH, IN THEIR OUTWARD APPEARANCE,
EXPRESS THEIR DIFFERENT FUNCTIONS. A HUMBLE BUILDING MATERIAL,
REINFORCED CONCRETE, WAS GIVEN NEW DIGNITY, AND INTERIOR
ENCLOSED SPACE WAS UNDERSTOOD AS THE ESSENCE OF
ARCHITECTURE.

THIS PROJECT WAS FINANCED JOINTLY BY THE NATIONAL PARK
SERVICE AND THE CHICAGO CHAPTER FOUNDATION OF THE
AMERICAN INSTITUTE OF ARCHITECTS. MEASURED AND DRAWN
DURING JULY AND AUGUST 1967 UNDER THE DIRECTION OF
JAMES C. MASSEY, CHIEF OF HABS, AND EARL H. REED, FAIA,
PROJECT SPONSOR, BY WESLEY SHANK (IOWA STATE UNIVERSITY),
PROJECT SUPERVISOR, AND STUDENT ASSISTANT ARCHITECTS
WHAYNE GRIFFIN (ILLINOIS INSTITUTE OF TECHNOLOGY), ALLAN
STEENHUSEN (IOWA STATE UNIVERSITY) AT THE CHICAGO
FIELD OFFICE, GLESSNER HOUSE. LELAND ROTH (YALE
UNIVERSITY), PROJECT HISTORIAN.

PHOTOSTATIC COPIES OF THE ARCHITECT'S ORIGINAL
WORKING DRAWINGS HAVE BEEN REFERRED TO. THE PRIN-
CIPAL DIMENSIONS HAVE BEEN CHECKED, AND DEPARTURES
FROM THE DRAWINGS HAVE BEEN TAKEN INTO ACCOUNT, SO
THAT THE BUILDING IS SHOWN AS IT WAS BUILT. THE PARTITIONS
RECENTLY ADDED AT BALCONY CLASSROOMS AND IN THE
BASEMENT BELOW THE AUDITORIUM ARE NOT SHOWN.

KENILWORTH ST.

GROVE ST.

LAKE STREET

KENILWORTH ST.

LOCATION PLAN

SCALE: 1"=50'-0"

NORTH

LOCATION MAP TAKEN FROM OAK PARK, ILLINOIS.
SANBORN MAP CO., NEW YORK, 1938, REVISED 1967. PLATE 103.

DRAWN BY: KELEAL HASSIN

HABS CHICAGO PROJECT IV 1967
OFFICE OF ARCHEOLOGY & HISTORIC PRESERVATION
UNDER DIRECTION OF THE NATIONAL PARK SERVICE,
UNITED STATES DEPARTMENT OF THE INTERIOR

NAME AND LOCATION OF STRUCTURE
UNITY TEMPLE
LAKE STREET AT KENILWORTH AVENUE, OAK PARK, ILLINOIS

SURVEY NO.
ILL. 1093

HISTORIC AMERICAN
BUILDINGS SURVEY
SHEET 1 OF 7 SHEETS

Location Plan, Unity Temple, Oak Park, Illinois—Wright (1906–7)
This plan shows the placement of Frank Lloyd Wright's Unity Temple on the corner of Lake Street and South Kenilworth Avenue in the Chicago suburb of Oak Park.

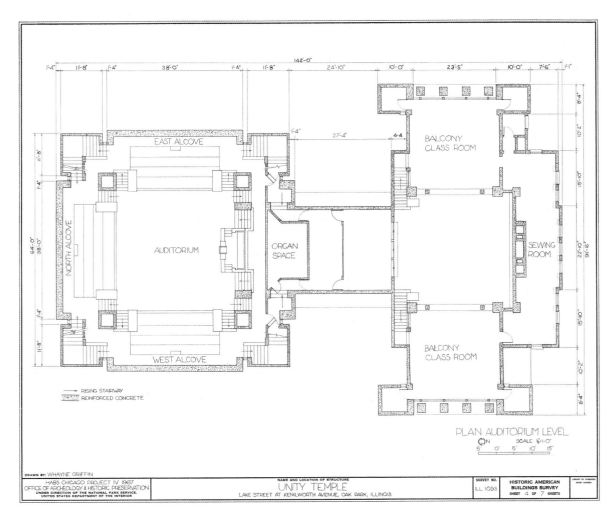

Unity Temple, Oak Park, Illinois—Wright (1906–7)

Designed by renowned architect Frank Lloyd Wright, Unity Temple was built between 1906 and 1908. It is one of the earliest public buildings constructed of concrete—poured in place and left exposed. Wright, who chose a cubist design for the church, described it as his "contribution to modern architecture." Unity Temple was designated a National Historic Landmark in 1971.

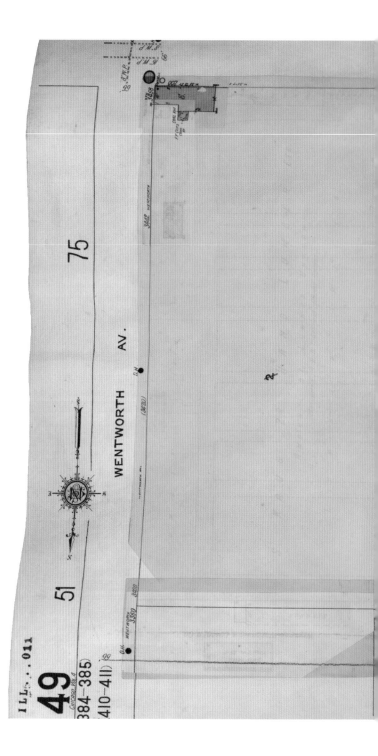

Comiskey Park—Sanborn Maps (1912)

This diagram shows Comiskey Park in 1912. Named for White Sox owner Charles A. Comiskey, it was the ballpark in which the Chicago White Sox played from 1910 to 1990. The modern concrete-and-steel stadium seated 32,000, including 7,000 in twenty-five-cent bleacher seats. The diagram indicates the upper deck in red.

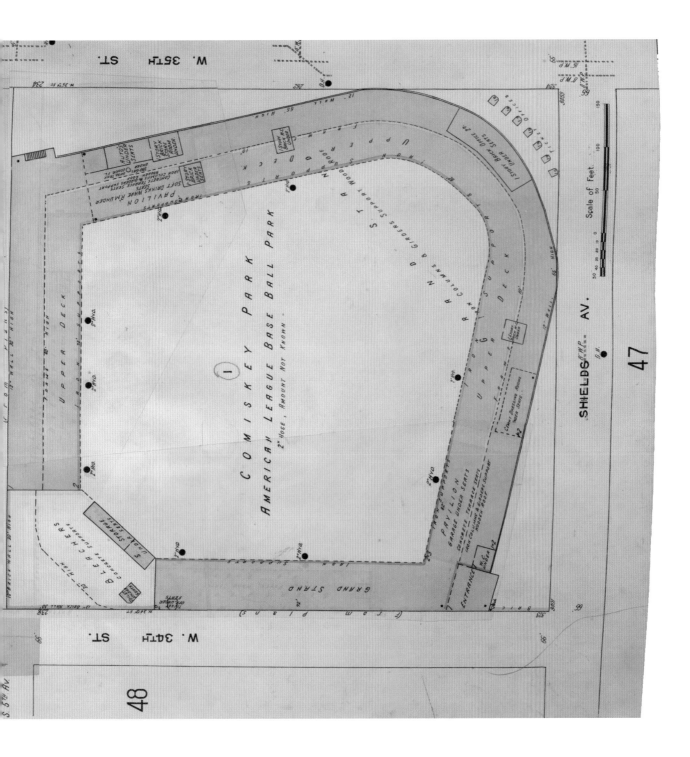

COMISKEY PARK

AMERICAN LEAGUE BASE BALL PARK

2" Hose, Amount Not Known -

W. 35TH ST.

W. 34TH ST.

SHIELDS AV.

47

48

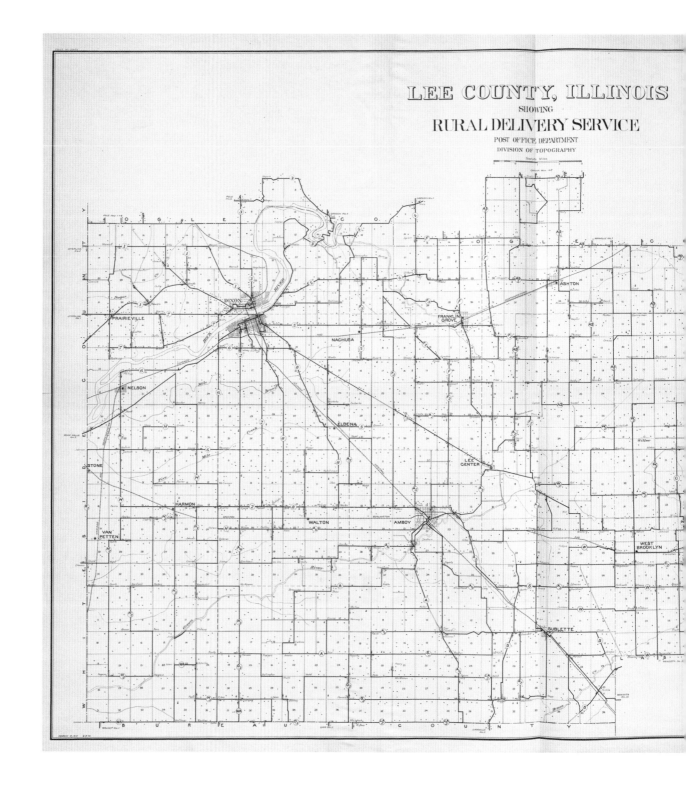

LEE COUNTY, ILLINOIS
SHOWING
RURAL DELIVERY SERVICE
POST OFFICE DEPARTMENT
DIVISION OF TOPOGRAPHY

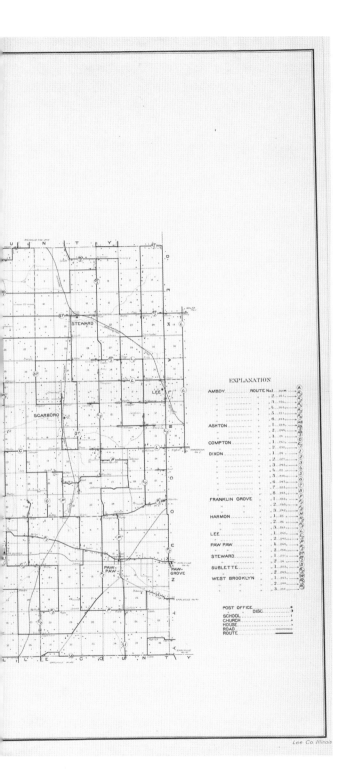

EXPLANATION

AMBOY .... ROUTE No.1 ....

ASHTON

COMPTON

DIXON

FRANKLIN GROVE

HARMON

LEE

PAW PAW

STEWARD

SUBLETTE

WEST BROOKLYN

POST OFFICE
SCHOOL .... DISC ....
CHURCH
HOUSE
ROAD
ROUTE

Lee Co. Illinois

Lee County, Illinois, showing rural delivery service—Post Office Department, Division of Topography (1912)

Lee County, Illinois, is located in the north-central part of the state. The earliest mail station within the county was Ogee's Ferry, established in 1829 and renamed Dixon's Ferry in 1833. Produced by the Post Office Department in 1912, this map labels ten cities and towns. Dixon, the county seat, is the site of the Lincoln Monument State Memorial, marking the spot where Abraham Lincoln joined the Illinois militia at Fort Dixon in 1832 during the Black Hawk War. Dixon was also the boyhood home of former U.S. president Ronald Reagan, who was born just a year before this map was published.

Chicago, central business section—
Reincke (ca. 1916)

In this bird's-eye view, oriented with north to the right, mapmaker Arno B. Reincke depicted Chicago's central business section as it appeared in 1916. It was in 1916 that Carl Sandburg's poem "Chicago" was published, containing his famous descriptions of the city as "Hog Butcher for the World" and "City of the Big Shoulders." That year, the shipping and entertainment venue Navy Pier opened and The Arts Club of Chicago was founded. Reincke's map is indexed for points of interest, including street names, parks, banks, Union Stock Yards, and such buildings as the Coliseum, Grand Central Station, City Hall, Marshall Field and Company, The Rookery, Union Station, the Grand Pacific Hotel, and the Monadnock Building. The rectangular section in the foreground is present-day Grant Park. Like most panoramic maps, this one is not drawn to scale.

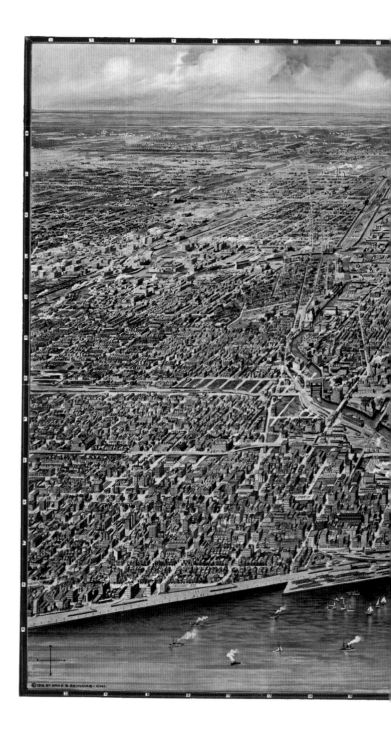

CHICAGO ~ CENTRAL BUSINESS SECTION

Indian Reservations west of the
Mississippi River—
Office of Indian Affairs (1923)

The original inhabitants of the area that is now Illinois included the Chickasaw, Dakota Sioux, Ho-Chunk (Winnebago), Illinois, Miami, and Shawnee. Tribes that migrated into Illinois after the Europeans arrived included the Delaware, Kickapoo, Ottawa, Potawatomi, Sac and Fox, and Wyandot. This map, published by the United States Office of Indian Affairs in 1923, indicates the locations of reservations to which Native Americans from Illinois and other states were forcibly removed during the nineteenth century. For example, the Peoria Tribe of Indians of Oklahoma is a confederation of Kaskaskia, Peoria, Piankesaw, and Wea Indians united into a single tribe in 1854. From their ancestral lands in Illinois, Michigan, Ohio, and Missouri, the Peorias were relocated first to Missouri, then to Kansas and, finally, to northeastern Oklahoma.

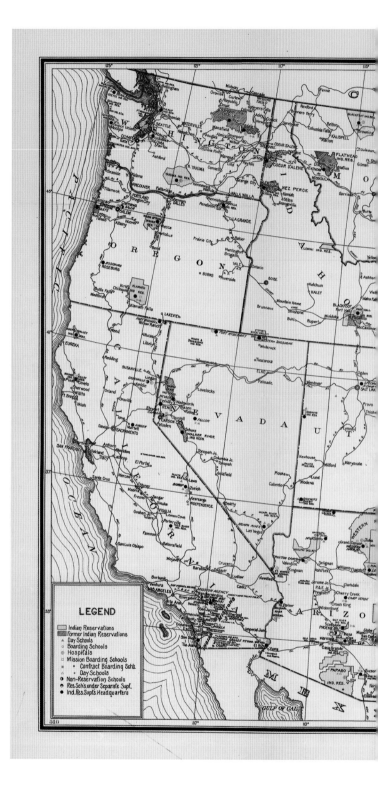

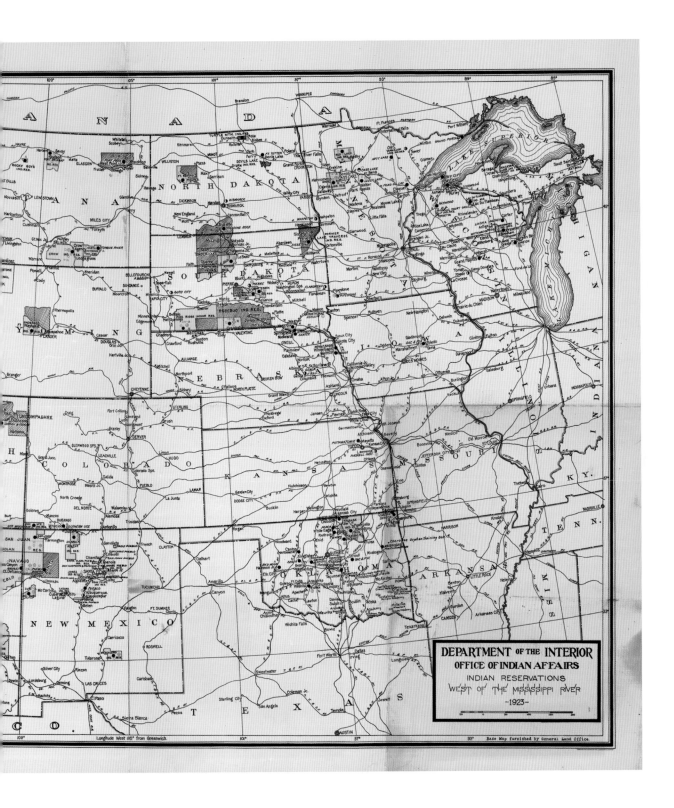

DEPARTMENT OF THE INTERIOR
OFFICE OF INDIAN AFFAIRS
INDIAN RESERVATIONS
WEST OF THE MISSISSIPPI RIVER
-1923-

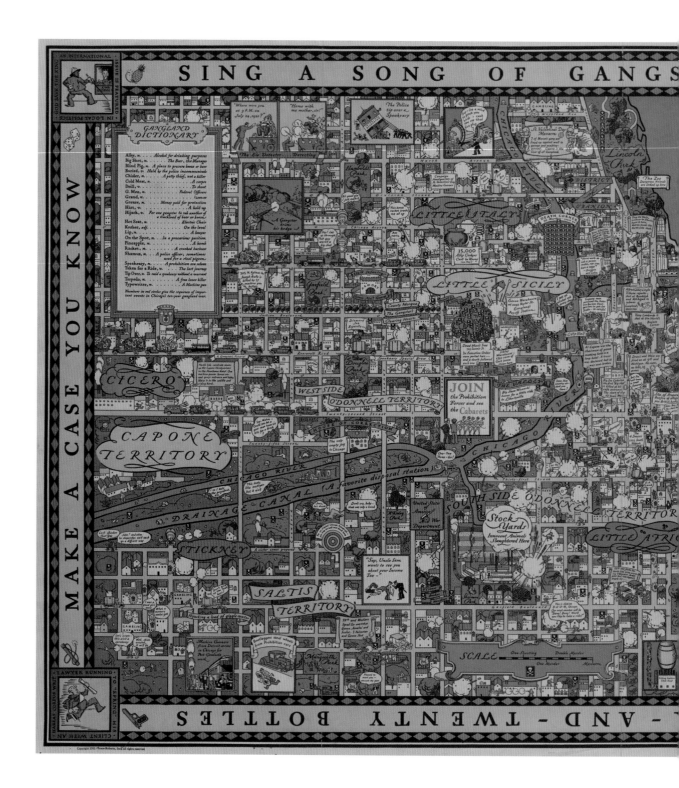

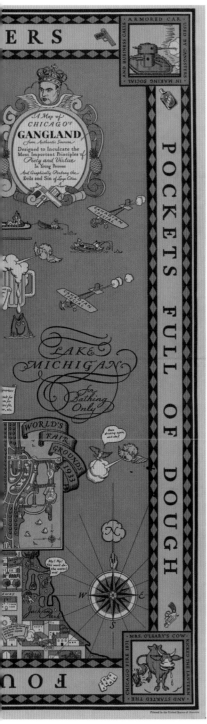

A Map of Chicago's Gangland from Authentic Sources. Designed to Inculcate the Most Important Principles of Piety and Virtue in Young Persons and Graphically Portray the Evils and Sin of Large Cities— Bruce-Roberts, Inc. (1931)

Printed in 1931, this map of Chicago includes a Gangland Dictionary that defines such terms as "Alky" (alcohol for drinking purposes), "Drill" (to shoot), and "Type-writer" (a machine gun). The territories of various gangsters are indicated, and key places of interest are labeled using "black humor." For example, the label for Union Stock Yards reads "Innocent Animals Slaughtered Here" and the Drainage Canal is labeled "a favorite disposal station." Two men are shown throwing a third man into the water.

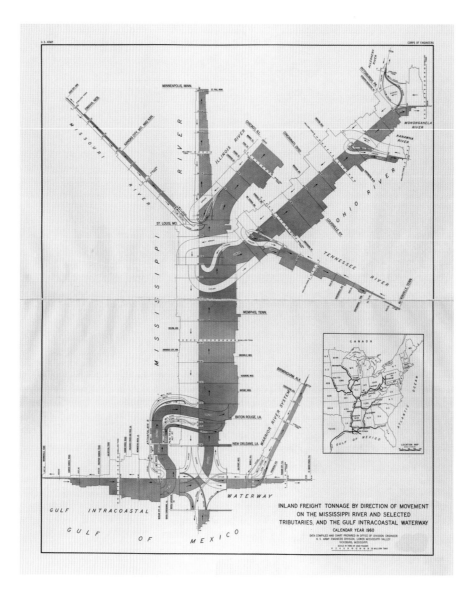

Inland freight tonnage by direction of movement on the Mississippi River and selected tributaries and the Gulf Intracoastal Waterway, calendar year 1960—Data compiled and chart prepared in Office of Division Engineer, U.S. Army Engineer Division, Lower Mississippi Valley

Created by the U.S. Army Corps of Engineers in 1960, this map illustrates the significant role played by Illinois waterways and cities in the movement of freight between the Gulf of Mexico and locations north, east, and west. The Illinois River is part of the Illinois Waterway, a system of rivers, lakes, and canals that connect the Great Lakes to the Gulf of Mexico via the Mississippi River. Primary cargoes carried on the Illinois Waterway include coal, chemicals, petroleum, corn, and soybeans.

Illinois after 1940

Long before the United States officially entered World War II, Illinois factories were committed to producing military equipment, weapons, and vehicles for the British and the French. B-29 Superfortress bomber engines rolled off the line at the Dodge factory in Chicago. Workers at the Elgin Watch Factory turned their attention to making time fuses for antiaircraft shells.

On December 8, 1941, Illinoisans listened along with the rest of the nation as President Franklin D. Roosevelt intoned: "I ask that the Congress declare that since the unprovoked and dastardly attack by Japan on Sunday, December 7, a state of war has existed between the United States and the Japanese empire."

Immediately the Illinois State Council of Defense (later the Illinois War Council) sprang into being. Before long, training facilities were set up across the state. The state fairgrounds in Springfield became an Air Force depot. Mechanics and radio operators were stationed in Chicago hotels. Millions of Illinois volunteers devoted themselves to organizations and causes such as Civil Defense, War Bonds, the USO (United Service Organizations), and the Red Cross.

As during World War I, thousands of African Americans came to Illinois from the South to find jobs in the newly expanded defense industry. Between 1940 and 1945 Chicago's African-American population increased by almost one hundred thousand.

A particularly significant contribution to the Allied cause occurred in 1942 at the University of Chicago. Under the west stand of Stagg Field, Enrico Fermi of Italy and his colleagues produced the first nuclear chain reaction. Fermi's work was essential to the development of the first atomic bomb, which the United States used against Japan to force an end to the war.

With the surrender of Germany in May 1945, and the surrender of Japan a few months later, the assimilation of veterans became a challenge for many states. In Illinois, veterans accounted for approximately one-eighth of the state's population. Housing proved to be a major concern, and Illinois veterans continued to face housing shortages well into the late 1940s.

In the area of education, schools consolidated and pooled their resources. Junior colleges were created and universities were expanded.

In agriculture, the number of small farms decreased after the war, and the farms that remained grew larger. Illinois was among the leading states in the production of corn, soybeans, and hogs. By this time, Illinois had also become a national leader in the radio and electronics industries. Disasters and labor disputes plagued Illinois coal mines during the 1940s and 1950s. In 1952 the Federal Coal Mine Safety Act updated safety laws and provided for more rigorous inspections.

Even as new, ultra-modern architectural styles flourished in Chicago, the city's residents flocked to the suburbs. Richard J. Daley, who was elected mayor in 1955, served an unprecedented six terms. Known as a prototypical "machine" politician, Daley initiated reforms and launched ambitious building projects, among them O'Hare International Airport. He was instrumental in making Chicago the "City that Works."

Daley's resolve was tested in 1968 during the Democratic National Convention. As people all over the world watched on television, protesters against the Vietnam War engaged in a violent free-for-all with Chicago police. Daley took a lot of heat for his hard-line response to the protests, but public opinion polls indicated considerable support for his actions.

In addition to the Vietnam War, the Civil Rights Movement made headlines in Illinois. In the late 1960s, Chicago emerged as the center for the Nation of Islam, an important black separatist movement. Chicago political and civil rights leader Jesse Jackson founded Operation PUSH (People United to Save [later Serve] Humanity) in 1971.

Women's rights took center stage in 1972 when Congress passed the Equal Rights Amendment (ERA). In order to go into effect, the amendment had to be ratified by thirty-eight states within seven years. The Illinois legislature did not ratify the ERA. Much more encouraging to proponents of women's rights was the election in 1979 of Jane Byrne as the first female mayor of Chicago.

That same year, Centralia native and future U.S. senator Roland Burris was elected comptroller, becoming the first African American to hold a statewide elective office in Illinois.

In 1980 the population of the state was 11,426,518. By then, the state had its first new constitution in one hundred years. The Abraham Lincoln Home in Springfield had been designated the first National Historic Site in Illinois. Chicago's skyline had become more impressive than ever, thanks to the world's tallest building: the 1,454-foot Sears Tower (later named Willis Tower).

Illinois had industrialized rapidly during the late 1800s while maintaining its position as a leading agricultural state. In the 1990s Illinois was once again challenged to keep up with the times as the United States changed from an industry-based economy to a service-based economy. The transition took a toll on Illinois, with its large number of blue-collar workers. In the 1990s labor problems involving thousands of employees at several plants earned the city of Decatur the nickname "Striketown U.S.A." By the early 2000s the economy of Illinois relied more on high-value-added services, such as financial trading, higher education, law, logistics, and medicine.

Farmers struggled with the effects of paving, flooding, strip mining, and other forms of development that drastically reduced the amount of available farmland. Farmers continued to produce record yields, but prices fluctuated wildly. Riverboat gambling was legalized in an effort to give the state's economy a boost. The population of Joliet increased dramatically during the 1990s, and many civic leaders credited the riverboat casinos for the growth.

In 1994 Chicago opened a renovated Navy Pier that featured a giant Ferris wheel, children's museum, stage pavilion, and retail shops. The Field Museum outbid rivals to acquire the most complete Tyrannosaurus Rex fossil yet discovered—named Sue in honor of the woman who discovered it.

As the new millennium drew near, immigrants from Mexico, India, Poland, and the Philippines congregated in the northern part of the state. Chicago's southwestern suburbs received a significant number of inhabitants from the Middle East. Immigrants from Latin America and Asia settled in the Chicago suburbs or downstate communities.

Life's ups and downs continued into the twenty-first century for Illinoisans. The year 2001 saw the groundbreaking ceremony for the Abraham Lincoln Presidential Library and Museum in Springfield. That same year, President George W. Bush declared ten Illinois counties to be disaster areas because of flooding along the upper Mississippi River.

In 2008 a U.S. senator from Illinois—Barack Obama—was elected forty-fourth president of the United States. It seemed somehow fitting that Obama, America's first African-American president, lived most of his adult life in the Land of Lincoln.

For Illinois, the twenty-first century—like many others—promises to be a time of celebrating achievements, learning lessons, and embracing change.

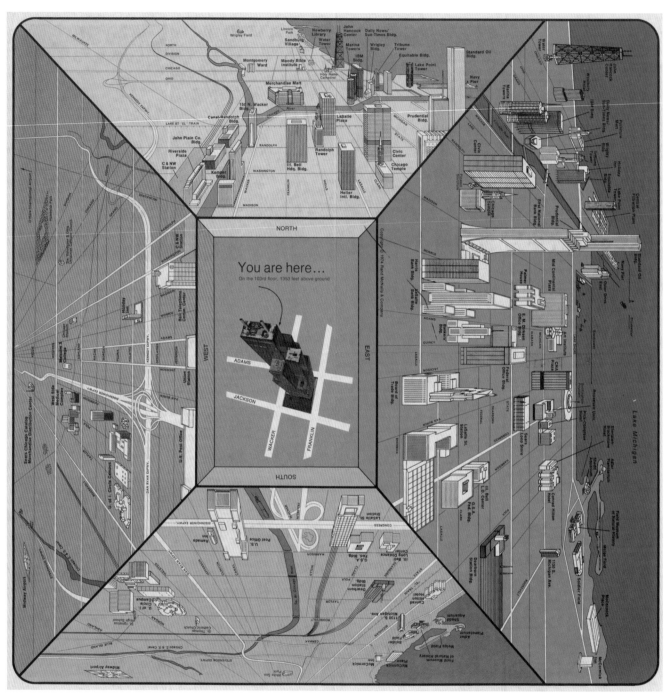

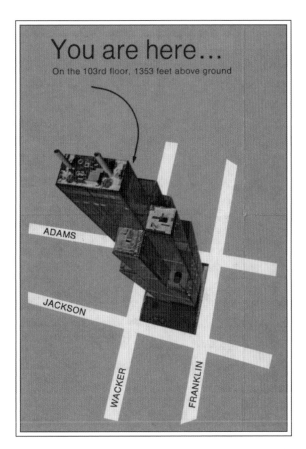

Sears Tower—Rand McNally and Company (1974)
The Sears Tower (changed to Willis Tower in 2009) was designed by Skidmore, Owings, and Merrill. Groundbreaking for construction took place in 1970. Construction of the 110-story building was completed in 1973, and the Skydeck on the 103rd floor officially opened in 1974. At that time, the tower was the world's tallest building. The Petronas Towers in Malaysia surpassed it in 1996, but only because of the spires atop the building. Based on roof height, the Sears Tower remained the tallest until 2003 when the Taipei Financial Center (Taipei 101) in Taiwan was completed.

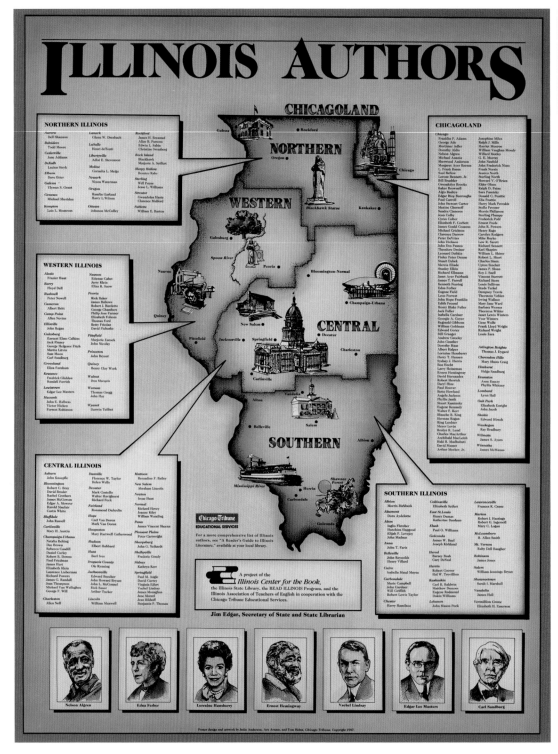

Ernest Hemingway

Illinois Authors—Anderson, Arnam, and Heinz (1987)

This map, a project of the Illinois Center for the Book, presents the state of Illinois divided into regions. Famous authors associated with each region are listed in boxes on either side. The text to the left of the map describes the authors pictured at the bottom and mentions some of their most famous works. Counties, major cities, and important buildings are also depicted on the map.

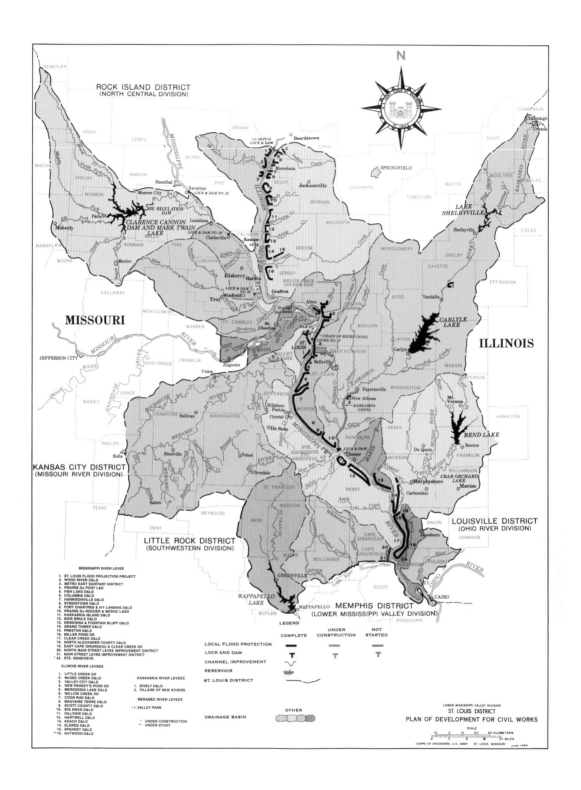

ROCK ISLAND DISTRICT
(NORTH CENTRAL DIVISION)

MISSOURI

JEFFERSON CITY

ILLINOIS

KANSAS CITY DISTRICT
(MISSOURI RIVER DIVISION)

LITTLE ROCK DISTRICT
(SOUTHWESTERN DIVISION)

LOUISVILLE DISTRICT
(OHIO RIVER DIVISION)

MEMPHIS DISTRICT
(LOWER MISSISSIPPI VALLEY DIVISION)

MISSISSIPPI RIVER LEVEE

1. ST. LOUIS FLOOD PROJECTION PROJECT
2. WOOD RIVER D&LD
3. METRO EAST SANITARY DISTRICT
4. PRAIRIE Du PONT L&D
5. FISH LAKE D&LD
6. COLUMBIA D&LD
7. HARRISONVILLE D&LD
8. STRINGTOWN D&LD
9. FORT CHARTRES & IVY LANDING D&LD
10. PRAIRIE Du ROCHER & MODOC L&DD
11. KASKASKIA ISLAND D&LD
12. BOIS BRULE D&LD
13. DEGOGNIA & FOUNTAIN BLUFF D&LD
14. GRAND TOWER D&LD
15. PRESTON D&LD
16. MILLER POND DD
17. CLEAR CREEK D&LD
18. NORTH ALEXANDER COUNTY D&LD
19. EAST CAPE GIRARDEAU & CLEAR CREEK DD
20. NORTH MAIN STREET LEVEE IMPROVEMENT DISTRICT
21. MAIN STREET LEVEE IMPROVEMENT DISTRICT
* 22. STE. GENEVIEVE

ILLINOIS RIVER LEVEES

1. LITTLE CREEK DD
2. McGEE CREEK D&LD
3. VALLEY CITY D&LD
4. NEW PANKEY'S POND DD
5. MEREDOSIA LAKE D&LD
6. WILLOW CREEK DD
7. COON RUN D&LD
8. MAUVAISE TERRE D&LD
9. SCOTT COUNTY D&LD
10. BIG SWAN D&LD
11. HILLVIEW D&LD
12. HARTWELL D&LD
13. KEACH D&LD
14. ELDRED D&LD
15. SPANKEY D&LD
** 16. NUTWOOD D&LD

KASKASKIA RIVER LEVEES

1. DIVELY D&LD
2. VILLAGE OF NEW ATHENS

MERAMEC RIVER LEVEES

* 1. VALLEY PARK

* UNDER CONSTRUCTION
** UNDER STUDY

LEGEND

	COMPLETE	UNDER CONSTRUCTION	NOT STARTED
LOCAL FLOOD PROTECTION			
LOCK AND DAM			
CHANNEL IMPROVEMENT			
RESERVOIR			
ST. LOUIS DISTRICT			

DRAINAGE BASIN .... OTHER

LOWER MISSISSIPPI VALLEY DIVISION
ST. LOUIS DISTRICT
PLAN OF DEVELOPMENT FOR CIVIL WORKS

SCALE

CORPS OF ENGINEERS, U.S. ARMY   ST. LOUIS, MISSOURI   JUNE 1995

Plan of development for civil works—Lower Mississippi Valley Division, St. Louis District, Corps of Engineers, U.S. Army (1995)

The U.S. Army Corps of Engineers, Mississippi Valley Division (MVD) is responsible for the navigation support and flood damage reduction on one of the largest inland waterway systems in the country. The St. Louis District, which encompasses 28,000 square miles, is almost equally divided between Missouri and Illinois. Its purpose is to maintain a proper and healthy balance of the varying uses of the region's waterways. The map, published in 1995, indicates the status or stage of completion of key elements of the plan: local flood protection, lock and dam, channel improvement, and reservoir. The map also includes an index to levees on the Mississippi, Illinois, and Kaskaskia Rivers.

Detail from map on pages 82 and 83

Conclusion

THE STORY OF ILLINOIS IS A STORY OF TRADITIONS, transitions, and transformations. At each point in the journey, the Prairie State has given its people the natural resources and variety of topographies they needed to create the world they desired.

The earliest known inhabitants built a community that covered six square miles near present-day Cahokia, Illinois. These members of what archaeologists call the Middle Mississippian culture created a highly developed civilization with the natural resources at their disposal.

For Indian tribes who arrived early in the sixteenth century, a desirable world included hunting as well as planting and harvesting crops. Illinois provided game animals, along with a climate and soil that nourished plants of many kinds.

In the minds of early French explorers such as Louis Jolliet, the fur trade was of foremost importance. His goal when he set out with Father Jacques Marquette in 1673 was to find the river the Indians called Misi Sipi ("big river"). The Illinois country provided the animals whose pelts kept the fur trade viable, but the French failed to colonize the area significantly during their ninety years of ownership.

British possession of the land that would one day be the state of Illinois ended with the Treaty of Paris, signed in 1783 at the end of the American Revolution. Not long after that, the U.S. Congress organized the Northwest Territory, which included the Illinois country. In 1800 Illinois became part of the Indiana Territory. During these transitions the land itself remained the same. Its hills, forests, ravines, lakes, rivers, woods, and prairies continued to support and nourish those who chose to live there.

Yet many potential settlers were not convinced that Illinois could provide the natural resources they needed to create a satisfactory life. Parts of Illinois remained uninhabited by whites due to the threat of malaria from mosquitoes and the fact that much of the prairie was treeless. How were they to build houses and barns without lumber? The scarcity of trees also suggested poor soil quality.

By the time the Illinois Territory was created in 1809, settlers had discovered that Illinois soil was in fact rich and fertile. Not only that, its continental climate (cold winters, warm summers, and frequent short fluctuations in temperature, humidity, cloudiness, and wind direction) was perfectly suited to raising crops.

In 1833 the United States acquired the last remaining Indian lands in Illinois through the Treaty of Chicago. The newest residents of Illinois began to transform the landscape. Once again, Illinois supplied the resources they required as they removed clay from the earth to make pottery and jugs and, later, firebrick. They mined coal. Trees were planted, towns were laid out, newspapers were founded, and schools and prisons were built. Before long, steamboats navigated rivers that once carried only canoes or rafts.

Chicago's location on Lake Michigan positioned it for an ever-increasing role in the nation's transportation system. By the middle of the nineteenth century, railroad tracks crisscrossed nearly every section of the state. Trains carried produce, coal, and mineral ore from Illinois to distant markets. During the Civil War, Illinois railroads were pressed into service on behalf of the Union cause. Illinois responded to every call for troops, even exceeding its quota.

In the late 1880s farms and farmers still held an essential place in the state's economy, but manufacturing increased markedly in importance. Many Illinoisans spent their working hours in factories instead of fields. Illinois farms and factories were called upon to provide food and supplies during both World War I and World War II. Families were called upon to provide soldiers.

After World War II, the number of small farms decreased, and the remaining farms grew larger. Illinois took the lead in the production of corn, soybeans, and hogs—but also excelled in the radio and electronics industries.

Today, Chicago retains its title as America's transportation hub. It is very likely that the city will be of central importance in the proposed development of a national high-speed rail network. The Port of Chicago serves as a link between the inland-river system, the Great Lakes, and the rest of the world.

While Chicago has long served as a focal point for the state and for the nation, other regions of the state have their own remarkable personalities, their own triumphs and tragedies worth noting.

During the eleventh century, Cahokia, located on the east bank of the Mississippi River across from St. Louis, was home to approximately fifteen thousand people. The prehistoric village was abandoned by around A.D. 1400. The courthouse in present-day Cahokia (St. Clair County) dates back to 1740. It served as an important center of political activity in the Old Northwest.

Southwest of Chicago on the Illinois River is Peoria (Peoria County), one of the oldest towns in the Prairie State. The land that became Peoria was first settled in 1680. Today the city serves as a regional hub for the primarily rural and agricultural center of the state.

Kaskaskia (Randolph County), in the southwestern part of the state, flourished in the 1700s. The village was the first capital of Illinois, but floods and erosion eventually obliterated the town, leaving a tiny island to represent the once-great center of French Illinois. In 1819 Congress donated land to the state for a new capital, and the town of Vandalia (Fayette County) was born. It was here that Abraham Lincoln began his political career. Lincoln was instrumental in getting the capital moved to Springfield (Sangamon County) in 1837.

The town of Bloomington (McClean County) in the central part of the state was chosen as the home for Illinois State Normal University. Founded in 1857, the college now known as Illinois State University was the first public institution of higher education in the state. The second-oldest public university in Illinois is the University of Illinois at Urbana-Champaign (Champaign County), which opened as Illinois Industrial University in 1868.

Galena (Jo Daviess County), in the far northwest corner of the state, was thriving in the days when Chicago was merely a trading post. During the "lead rush" of the 1800s, prospectors and miners flocked to Galena from the east as well as from foreign countries. Another northwestern city, Rock Island (Rock Island County), began as an Illinois Indian village on the Mississippi River and grew into a center for the agricultural implements industry.

As the twenty-first century progresses, Illinois lawmakers will no doubt continue to wrestle with the need to promote economic development while protecting the state's natural resources. A state law passed in 2007 mandating renewable energy growth has already led to an expansion in wind energy development. Illinois has the strong winds, acreage, and infrastructure needed to utilize this form of energy efficiently.

Whatever the future brings, the twenty-first state can count on the enthusiasm, persistence, and resourcefulness that has characterized each generation of the area's inhabitants. From north to south, from big city to small town, from factory to farm—the Prairie State has the natural and human resources necessary to build a bright future.

Acknowledgments

First on the list is Erin Turner whose vision and creative editorial participation make these books a joy for me; without her this audacious project would not be the permanent achievement it is destined to be. On our Globe Pequot Press team I treasure Julie Marsh (indefatigable project manager), Sheryl Kober (visionary designer–Oh, these vellum jackets!), Lori Enik (digital file miracle worker), and Casey Shain (layout and Photoshop artist). The patience, organizational skills, and technical wizardry of my gifted colleague Aimee Hess are essential to my survival, as is the research assistance I receive from the masters in the Library of Congress Geography and Map Division: John Hebert (its Chief), Cynthia Cook, John Hessler, Charlotte Houtz, Michael Klein, Stephen Paczolt, and Edward Redmond.

—Vincent Virga

In addition to Erin Turner, Julie Marsh, and the rest of the Globe Pequot Press team, I am particularly grateful to the Bloomington Public Library and to Roger Biles of Illinois State University, whose book *Illinois: A History of the Land and Its People* was of critical importance to me in my research for this book.

—Scotti Cohn

All maps come from Library of Congress Geography and Map Division, Washington, D.C., 20540-4650 unless otherwise noted. To order reproductions of Library of Congress items, please contact the Library of Congress Photoduplication Service, Washington, D.C., 20540-4570 or (202) 707-5640.

Page viii Ruysch, Johann. Universalior cogniti orbis tabula. In Claudius Ptolemeus, *Geographia*. Rome, 1507. G1005.1507 Vault.

Page ix Waldseemüller, Martin. Universalis cosmographia secundum Ptholomaei traditionem et Americi Vespucii alioru que lustrations. St. Dié, France?, 1507. G3200 1507 .W3 Vault.

Pages 4–5 (detail, page ii) Joliet, Louis. Nouvelle decouverte de plusieurs nations dans la Nouvelle France en l'année 1673 et 1674. From the Jesuit Relations, vol. 59, p. facing 86. Original version, 1674. G3300 1674 .J6 1896 TIL.

Pages 6–7 Marquette, Jacques. Carte de la decouverte faite l'an 1673 dans l'Amerique Septentrionale, Liebaux Sculp, 1681. G159 .T38, G4042.M5.

Page 8 Franquelin, Jean Baptiste Louis, The Mississippi, ca. 1682. G4042.M5 1682 .F7 Vault: Kohl 229.

Pages 12–13 Carte de l'Amerique Septentrionale: depuis le 25, jusqu'au 65° deg. de latt. & environ 140, & 235 deg. de longitude, par Iean Baptiste Louis Franquelin, hydrographe du roy, à Québec en Canada. Copied between 1909 and 1910 from the original 1688 ms. in the Archives du dépôt des cartes et plans de la marine. G3300 1688 .F7 Vault Oversize.

Pages 14–15 Lahontan, Louis Armand de Lom d'Arce, baron de. Carte de la rivière Longue: et de quelques autres, qui se dechargent dans le grand fleuve de Missisipi [*sic*] ... ; Carte que les Gnacsitares: ont dessine sur des paux de cerfs ... La Haye, Netherlands, 1703. G4050 1703 .L3 Vault.

Page 16 Pittman, Philip. A draught of the Missisipi [*sic*] River from Balise up to Fort Chartres. London. Printed for J. Nourse, 1770. F352 .P68 G4042.M5.

Pages 20–21 Le Rouge, Georges-Louis. Partie occidentale de la Virginie, Pensylvanie, Maryland, et Caroline Septle. la rivière d'Ohio, et toutes celles qui s'y jettent, partie de la Rivière Mississippi, tout le cours de la rivière de Illinois, le Lac Erie, partie des Lacs Huron et Michigan &. toutes les contrées qui bordent ces lacs et rivières, par Hutchins, capitaine anglais. Paris: Chez Le Rouge, 1781. G3707.O5 1781 .L4 Vault: Roch 49.

Page 22–23 Fielding, I. A map of the United States of America, as settled by the peace of 1783. London, Decr. 1, 1783. G3700 1783 .F52 TIL Vault.

Pages 24–25 Les États Unis de l'Amérique septentrionale, partie occidentale. Par Rigobert Bonne, ingenieur hydrographe de la marine. André, sculp. Paris, 1788. G4042.M5 1788 .B6 Low 676.

Pages 26–27 North America from the Mississippi River to the Pacific, between the 35th and 60th parallels of latitude, 179-?. G3300 179- .N6 TIL Vault: L&C i.

Pages 28–29 Plan of the N.W. frontier, from Governor William Clarke, ca. 1813. G4042.M5 1813 .C5 Vault: Jackson 10.

Pages 30–31 A map exhibiting all the new discoveries in the interior parts of North America, inscribed by permission to the honorable governor and company of the adventurers of England trading into Hudsons Bay, in testimony of their liberal communications to their most obedient and very humble servant Aaron Arrowsmith, hydrographer to H.R.H. the Prince of Wales, January 1st 1795; Puke, sc. London: A. Arrowsmith, 1814. G3300 1814 .A7.

Pages 32–33 Carey, Mathew. The Upper Territories of the United States. From Carey's General Atlas, 1814. G4070 1814 .C3.

Page 34 Map of Illinoise [sic], constructed from the surveys in the General Land Office and other documents by John Melish. Philadelphia: John Melish, 1818? G4100 1818 .M4 Vault.

Page 35 Hydrographical basin of the upper Mississippi River from astronomical and barometrical observations, surveys, and information. By J. N. Nicollet in the years 1836, 37, 38, 39, and 40; assisted in 1838, 39 & 40, by Lieut. J. C. Fremont, of the Corps of Topographical Engineers under the superintendence of the Bureau of the Corps of Topographical Engineers and authorized by the War Department. Washington: Published by order of the U.S. Senate, 1843. G4042.M5 1843 .N5 Vault.

Pages 36–37 Mendel, Edward. Map showing the position of Chicago in connection with the North West & the principal lines of rail roads, canals, navigable streams and leakes, together with the most important towns, and their distances from Chicago. Chicago, 185-. G4061.P3 185- .M4 RR 115.

Page 38 Ensign, Bridgman & Fanning. Rail road and county map of Illinois showing its internal improvements 1854. New York, 1854. G4100 1854 .E5 RR 202.

Page 39 D.B. Cooke & Co.'s railway guide for Illinois shewing all the stations with their respective distances connecting with Chicago. Chicago, 1855. G4101.P3 1855 .D15 RR 203.

Page 44 Hall, Edward S. Western border states. Waters and son Eng. N.Y., New York: H. H. Lloyd & Co., ca. 1861. 3700 1861 .H3 CW 12.7.

Page 45 Sectional map of the state of Illinois: especially exhibiting the exact boundaries of counties as established by law and the general topography of the state as towns, streams, lakes, ponds, bluffs, rail-roads, state-& common-roads & tc. also the main coal field, mineral districts, outcrops of coalbanks, mines & tc., compiled & drawn from the government—state—geological—topographical and many other most authentic documents of Leopold Richter, State Topographer, Springfield, Ill.; engraved on stone and printed by Leopold Gast, Brother & Co., St. Louis, Mo., 1861. G4100 1861 .R5 RR 205.

Pages 46–47 Bird's eye view of junction of the Ohio & Mississippi Rivers, showing Cairo and part of the southern states. Drawn from nature and lith. by John Bachmann. New York: A. Rumpf, 1861. G4041.A35 1861 .B3 CW 1.5.

Pages 48–49 (detail, page 40) Map shewing [sic] the several routes proposed for the passage of gunboats to the Lakes via: Erie and Oswego Canal; Champlain [Canal]; Illinois River and Chicago [Canal]; Wisconsin, Green Bay [Canal]. Prepared by S. H. Sweet, Dep. State Engr. and Surveyor. Albany, N.Y., Lith. of C. Van Benthuysen, 1862. G3711.P5 1862 .S9 CW 33.

Page 50–51 Speidel, C. Rock Island Barracks, Ill. Lith. C. Vogt. H. Lambach sct., Davenport Io., 1864. G4104. R6:2R6 1864 .S6 CW 215.

Page 52 Geographical history of the rail road regiment, 89th regiment of Illinois vols. infantry [1862–1865]. Platted and compiled from U.S. Coast Survey maps, by Isaac N. Merritt. Lithographed by Chas. Shober, Chicago, ca. 1860. G3861.S5 18-- .M4 CW 77.6.

Page 53 Sketch and plan for a fortification opposite Paducah, Ky., 1864. G3954.P2S5 1864 .S5 Vault: CW 225.

Pages 58–59 (detail, page 54) Springfield, Illinois 1867. Drawn from nature by A. Ruger. Chicago: Chicago Lithographing Co., 1867. G4104.S5A3 1867 .R8 Rug 35.

Pages 60–61 Bird's eye view of Manteno, Kankakee County, Illinois, 1869. Drawn by A. Ruger. Chicago: Merchant's Lithogr. Co., 1869. G4104.M26A3 1869 .R8 Rug 23.

Pages 62–63 Bird's eye view of the city of Moline, Rock Island County, Illinois, 1869. Drawn by A. Ruger. Chicago Lithogr. Co. Madison, Wis.: Ruger & Stoner, 1869. G4104.M6A3 1869 .R8 Rug 24.

Page 64–65. Bird's eye view of Young America, Warren County, Illinois, 1869. Drawn by A. Ruger. Chicago Lith. Co. Madison, Wis.: Ruger & Stoner, 1869. G4104.Y7A3 1869 .R8 Rug 38.

Pages 66–67 Bird's eye view of the city of Urbana, Champaign County, Illinois, 1869. Drawn by A. Ruger. Chicago: Chicago Lithogrg. Co., 1869. G4104.U7A3 1869 .R8 Rug 37.

Pages 68–69 Map showing the line of the Louisville, New Albany, and St. Louis Air Line Railroad and its connections. New York: G.W. & C.B. Colton & Co., 1872. G3701.P3 1872 .G15 RR 451.

Pages 70–71 The City of Chicago as it was before the great conflagration of October 8th, 9th, & 10th, 1871. Chicago, Ill.?: W. Flint, ca. 1872. G4104.C6A3 1871 .C5 MLC.

Pages 72–73 Map Showing the Burnt District in Chicago. Published for the benefit of the Relief Fund by 3rd Edition. St. Louis: The R.P. Studley Company, 18--.

Pages 74–75 The City of Chicago, sketched & drawn on stone by Parsons & Atwater. New York: Published by Currier & Ives, ca. 1874. Prints & Photographs Division, Library of Congress. LC-DIG-ppmsca-08968.

Pages 76–77 Heubach, Emil. New rail road map of the United States and the Dominion of Canada, showing the Chicago, Rock Island and Pacific R.R.; the great overland route and short line to the west and southwest. Chicago, 1879. G3701.P3 1879 .H42 RR 379.

Pages 78–79 Elgin, Kane Co., Illinois 1880. Del. by A. B. Upham. Chicago: Shober & Carqueville, ca. 1880. G4104.C6A3 1890 .R3 TIL.

Pages 80–81 Rascher, Charles. Rascher's birds eye view of the Chicago packing houses & union stock yards, 1890. G4104.C6A3 1890 .R3 TIL.

Page 82–83 (detail, page 110) Bird's eye view of the World's Columbian Exposition, Chicago, 1893. Rand McNally and Company, 1893. G4104.C6:2W95 1893 .R2 TIL.

Pages 84–85 All elevated trains in Chicago stop at the Chicago Rock Island and Pacific Railway Station, only one on the Loop, [prepared for] Chicago, Rock Island & Pacific Railway. Chicago, Ill.: Poole Bros., ca. 1897. G4104.C6P33 1897 .P6.

Pages 86–87 Champion, Willis J. Birds Eye View of the Elevated Railroads and the Parks and Boulevards of Chicago, 1908.

Page 88 Wright, Frank Lloyd. Location plan, Unity Temple, Oak Park, Illinois, from the Historic American Building Survey, 1906–7. Prints & Photographs Division, Library of Congress. HABS ILL,16-OAKPA, 3-1.

Page 89 Wright, Frank Lloyd. Unity Temple, Oak Park, Illinois, from the Historic American Building Survey, 1906–7. Prints & Photographs Division, Library of Congress. HABS ILL,16-OAKPA, 3-4.

Pages 90–91 Comiskey Park, 1912. Sanborn Maps, Volume 4, sheet 49.

Pages 92–93 Lee County, Illinois, showing rural delivery service, Post Office Department, Division of Topography. Post Office Dept., 1912. G4103.L5P8 1912 .U5.

Pages 94–95 Reincke, Arno B. Chicago, central business section. Chicago, ca. 1916. G4104.C6A3 1916 .R4.

Pages 96–97 Indian Reservations west of the Mississippi River. United States. Office of Indian Affairs, 1923. G4051.E1 1923 .U5 TIL.

Pages 98–99 A Map of Chicago's Gangland from Authentic Sources. Designed to Inculcate the Most Important Principles of Piety and Virtue in Young Persons and Graphically Portray the Evils and Sin of Large Cities. Bruce-Roberts, Inc., 1931.

Page 100 Inland freight tonnage by direction of movement on the Mississippi River and selected tributaries and the Gulf Intracoastal Waterway: calendar year 1960, data compiled and chart prepared in Office of Division Engineer, U.S. Army Engineer Division, Lower Mississippi Valley. Vicksburg, Miss.: U.S. Army Engineer Division, Lower Mississippi Valley, 1960. G4042.M5P53 1960 .U5.

Pages 104–5 Sears Tower. Chicago: Rand McNally and Company, 1974. G4104 .C6A3 1974 .R3.

Pages 106–7 Anderson, Julie; Arnam, Arn; and Heinz, Tom. Illinois Authors. Chicago: Chicago Tribune Educational Services, 1987. G4101.E65 1987 .A5.

Pages 108–9 Plan of development for civil works, Lower Mississippi Valley Division, St. Louis District, Corps of Engineers, U.S. Army. St. Louis, Mo.: The District, 1995. G4042.M5N22 1995 .U5.

About the Authors

VINCENT VIRGA earned critical praise for *Cartographia: Mapping Civilization* and coauthored *Eyes of the Nation: A Visual History of the United States* with the Library of Congress and Alan Brinkley. Among his other books are *The Eighties: Images of America*, with a foreword by Richard Rhodes; *Eisenhower: A Centennial Life*, with text by Michael Beschloss; and *The American Civil War: 365 Days*, with Gary Gallagher and Margaret Wagner. He has been hailed as "America's foremost picture editor" for having researched, edited, and designed nearly 150 picture sections in books by authors including John Wayne, Jane Fonda, Arianna Huffington, Walter Cronkite, Hillary Clinton, and Bill Clinton. Virga edited *Forcing Nature: Trees in Los Angeles*, photographs by George Haas for Vincent Virga Editions. He is the author of six novels, including *Gaywyck, Vadriel Vail*, and *A Comfortable Corner*, as well as publisher of ViVa Editions. He has a Web site through the Author's Guild at www.vincentvirga.com.

SCOTTI McAULIFF COHN grew up in Springfield, Illinois. Some of her favorite childhood memories include visits to Lincoln's home and tomb and to New Salem, where Lincoln lived as a young adult. Today Scotti lives in Bloomington, Illinois, where she works as a freelance writer and copy editor. Her other books for Globe Pequot Press include *Chicago Curiosities, It Happened in Chicago, It Happened in North Carolina, More Than Petticoats: Remarkable North Carolina Women, Beyond Their Years: Stories of 16 Civil War Children*, and *Liberty's Children: Stories of 11 Revolutionary War Children*. She is also the author of two children's picture books: *One Wolf Howls* (2009) and *Big Cat, Little Kitty* (2011). Her Web site is located at www.scotticohn.com.